EMERGENCY GUIDE!

Privy information for you to use quickly abroad

Squat toilet: Where do you sit? Where do your feet go?

Y ou're in **Venice** when you quickly have to answer a call of nature. You have been ushered into a public toilet. But all you see is a sort of hole in the floor — the formidable squat toilet. What do you do?

Quick, turn to **Page 2.**

In **Turkey**, you look around but there is no toilet tissue. Aghast, you see only a small bowl with water in it. Thoughts of how to use the pages of this book come to mind. Instead, look for ways to use the water — and which hand to use.

Bowl of water — for what?

Deftly refer to **Page 5.**

Latrine etiquette: What's involved?

You are in **China** and you feel a familiar, urgent need. Nearby is only the village latrine. You enter, and there are people squatting over what looks like a long trench. What is the appropriate etiquette here?

Raise your book quickly and turn to **Page 30.**

You are on safari in darkest **Africa.** The guides warn you not to leave your tent after night falls — and now you know why as you hear nearby lions snarl. Yet nature calls. What do you do (and you *do* need to do something)?

Call on **Page 18.**

London coin-operated street toilet

On the streets of **London**, you feel the urge. In front of you, on a street corner, is an unfamiliar-looking small building. Yes, it's a public toilet, and a very modern one, but it looks strange. You put some coins in the slot and step inside —and it is still strange. Good grief! What next?

For relief, *see* **Page 54.**

You are in **Spain** — but where's the toilet? You have a problem in that you don't speak or understand the language. What can you do?

Ole! Quickly turn to **Page 67.**

The formidable bidet: How do you use it?

It's springtime in **Paris** and in your hotel bathroom, there are two nearly identical porcelain receptacles on the floor. One of these is a bidet. You are cultured; you are wise. And you are game. So how do you use it?

To get flushed with success,
check out **Page 57.**

You are in **Amsterdam** and about to enter a public toilet. You see an International Toilet Sign for men and for women. But you don't remember which sign you are under. What next?

Are you this?

Or this?

Don't take another step
until you check **Page 76.**

GOING ABROAD

SECOND EDITION

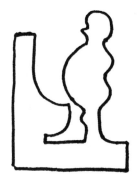

How to answer the call of nature
anywhere in the world. A must for
travelers wherever they, er, go!

E V A   N E W M A N

MARLOR PRESS, INC.

Saint Paul, Minnesota

GOING ABROAD
Second Edition

A Marlin Bree Book
Published by Marlor Press, Inc.

Copyright 1997, 2000 by Eva Newman
Illustrations by the author
Cover design by MacLean & Tuminelly

Distributed to the book trade in the U.S.A. by
Independent Publishers Group, Chicago

ISBN 1-892147-03-3

Manufactured in the United States of America

Disclaimer: This book is intended only as a general guide to various toilet facilities throughout the world. Readers should check individual facilities and services to meet their own needs and use their own judgment and discretion as to availability, safety and suitability. If they have a physical problem, readers are strongly cautioned to consult with their physician or other health care professional before engaging in the exercises or situations described in this book and to adapt the usage for their own needs and limitations. This book is sold without warranties of any kind, express or implied, and the publisher and the author disclaim any responsibility for safety, services, availabilities, prevailing conditions, agreements, damages, or loss or injury or any special, incidental, contingent or consequential damages of any kind. Not responsible for omissions and errors. Purchase of this book constitutes acceptance of these terms.

M A R L O R   P R E S S ,   I N C .
4304 Brigadoon Drive   Saint Paul, Minnesota 55126

CONTENTS

THE
BEGINNING

Whether you refer to it as the can, john, poet's corner, little boy's or girl's room, powder room, chamber of commerce, reading room, throne or some other amusing or euphemistic term, the reference usually brings to mind an object upon which one sits in order to conduct a necessary function of elimination common to everyone.

Whenever the subject of toilets is discussed with fellow travelers, an evening of entertaining stories usually follows. Even at parties in the United States, the subject will bring eager comments from the shyest guest. The adventures related are usually misadventures, which occurred because of lack of understanding or acceptance of unfamiliar toilet facilities.

After twenty-five years of world travel, usually using non-first class facilities, I've had extensive encounters with toilets that are strange by American standards. The purpose of this book is to demystify obstacles that have kept people from traveling to where they cannot instantly find Western-type (sit) toilets.

This attitude definitely prevents travel to many out-of-the way places in the world. I encourage readers to carefully examine their attitudes toward their contemporary toilet habits. We have an almost Victorian attitude toward the normal human elimination of bodily wastes.

Going Abroad, I hope, will help prepare readers for some of the different toilets and customs to be found in their travels around the world — and make the encounters easier.

— Eva Newman

HOW
TO
SQUAT

*Common marketplace
resting position
in Asian countries*

Toilet facilities fall into general categories, squat and sit. Surprisingly to many Westerners, a large part of the world actually prefers the position of squatting.

Just what is a squat toilet and how is it used? The example illustrated is the kind of squat toilet frequently encountered. Although such toilets are sometimes referred to as a "hole in the ground," you can see that this is not true.

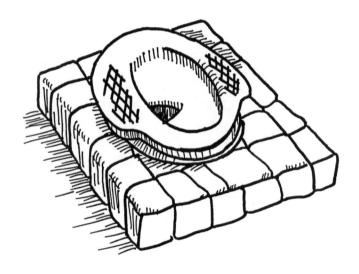

Ceramic Squat Toilet

Now that you've seen it, what do you do? First learn the physical act of squatting. Squatting is something Americans seldom do.

Therefore, a few weeks before your trip, you will need to begin practicing. Women, for apparent reasons, will have to squat more often and so may want to practice more.

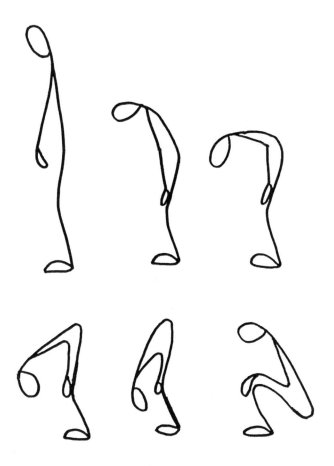

Analysis of a proper squat

To squat, you will need to spread your feet apart and concentrate on your balance. The proper squat, as shown in the diagram, begins by bending the upper portion of the body forward for a proper distribution of weight. Then simply lower yourself by bending your legs. You will come to rest quite naturally on your legs and haunches, with your joints taking the weight. Properly assumed, the position is pleasant, natural, and effortless.

Getting to that point, however, does take practice. It's a good idea, if you are going to a part of the world that has squat toilets, to practice the squatting position. At the beginning of training, take a few moments to practice going down, balancing yourself, then getting up. Take your time and get the feel for the position. Remember that it's a natural one for most of the world. You should feel comfortable going into a squat — and remaining there to do your essential business.

Of course, if you have a knee problem or other physical ailment or handicap, consult your physician before proceeding with the squat.

While learning to squat, you will discover clothing can be a problem. For women, full skirts are easier to handle than pants. Just hold the skirt around your waist. Skirts are not only cooler in hot climates, but can become a private outhouse in an emergency situation. As you will see, men do not have all the advantages of anatomy in these toilet maneuvers.

If you wear pants, roll the bottom half of the legs to your knees. Next, lower the top of your pants to your knees. Squat. If you are in proper squat position, the knees will hold your pants in place. Underpants are dealt with by treating them in the same way as long pants: lower them to your knees. You do not want them around your ankles.

At this point in your training, you will discover most of the items in your pockets will have left your pockets and would now be in the toilet had there been one. Let me assure you that would be a most unpleasant and unfortunate event. Therefore, check your pockets before squatting — and temporarily remove the contents.

Now, to the next matter: your aim. Frankly, aim in sit toilets is of little importance. Your rear is safely enclosed by the toilet seat and toilet bowl. However, while using squat toilets, your rear is surrounded by your legs, feet and shoes. I think you can see this can be cause for alarm unless you are properly prepared. Ladies, at this point, consider the perils of panty hose and high heels. Your aim can spell success or failure.

Concentration and practice are essential. Be advised that to achieve good aim is not impossible. Begin to practice every time nature calls. Try aiming for a particular area in the toilet. Start this practice several weeks before your trip.

What to use instead of toilet tissue

Now you can squat and aim, but what about the final step? You look about, but there is no toilet paper. This is because squat cultures always seem to use water instead of paper for cleansing the bottom.

Using water and the hand instead of paper is the next step to learn. Practice this step in old clothes, preferably similar to what you will wear on your trip. Remember that this is how more than half the world does it.

Get into the bathtub or shower. Take with you a plastic cup or a small pan with a handle. Brightly colored plastic containers are commonly found in squat toilets around the world. Note that the container used must be unbreakable.

This is because, should the container unexpectedly leave your hand, glass splinters in your bottom are decidedly undesirable.

Next, fill the container with water. You can start practicing with warm water, but in reality you will probably never have warm water available. You may as well get used to cold water as soon as you can. Hold the container in your right hand and get into the squat position.

At this point, a variation in style can occur according to personal preference. You can use your left hand either in front of the rear, or in back of your rear, for cleansing. A lot depends on where in the world you are going.

For example, in India I was instructed to place the left hand behind my rear. In other words, take your left hand while in the squat position and place it behind your left leg — more or less near your bottom.

In Southeast Asia I was instructed to place my left hand around the front of my bent left leg and under my bottom. This I found more difficult.

In either case, hold the container in your right hand and pour water into your left hand (wherever it is). Then splash and cleanse the necessary area as you pour.

Again, some practice is required.

This last part of the squat procedure, the cleansing act, is the most unnerving for Americans. If it is done well, there should be no problems.

In hot climates you may even experience a cooling and refreshing relief. You will probably find it much more soothing than using toilet paper after a bout of diarrhea.

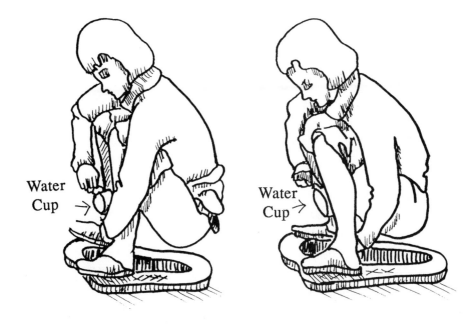

*Squat position
with hand in front*

*Squat position
with hand in back*

Bear in mind, a large segment of our fellow humans prefer
this method of cleansing with water. It may be clear to you
now why some cultures consider social use of the left hand
impolite. Left-handed people can be confronted with
problems of etiquette in these countries.

Practice rising from the squatting position, for standing
again after squatting can be a problem. I have found
the following method of standing easiest for me. I
straighten my legs before lifting the upper part of my
body. Then I roll the upper body from the waist until I am
upright again. (See diagram on page 9.)

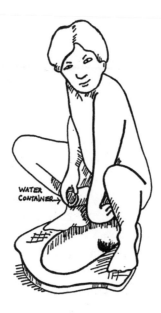

Squat position with washing hand in front

Shake yourself and wash your hands. You will by now be aware that washing your hands well is very necessary. The water for washing may be from the same source as that used for the toilet function. There is seldom soap.

I suggest you carry your own soap or wash-and-dries treated with anti-bacterial solution. Another suggestion is to use soap leaves. Soap leaves are very thin slices of soap in the shape of two-inch by three-inch rectangles; they come in packets of fifteen to twenty leaves and are lightweight and compact for easy transport. They frequently can be purchased in gift shops in the United States.

For those who feel that soap will not do an adequate cleaning job, the answer may be not to dirty your hands at all. Some people use disposable latex gloves. Of course, you will now be confronted with the problem of disposal of the gloves. Trash containers are often difficult to find.

Or you can use what my camping friend uses for a no-hands approach: an empty washing detergent squirt bottle. Fill it with water, aim, and squirt. It is accurate and controlled.

Careful cleaning of your hands before eating can be a big help in preventing illness. While on safari in Africa, we were not allowed to even get our food until we had washed our hands in a special solution; no one became ill on that three-week trip in the wilderness. In addition, I was told that clipping your nails short will help keep hands clean. The space under the nails is a hiding place for germs.

Since there is bound to be some water spilled during the final steps of your cleansing procedure, nonskid shoes are helpful in preventing treacherous excursions into the toilet. Thick soles on the shoes will help raise you above the spilled water and prevent wet feet.

Sequence for arising from squatting position. The legs are straightened with the upper body bent forward. Then the upper body is lifted upright. Experiment to find what method works best for you.

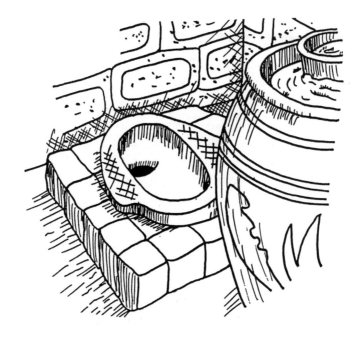

Modern squat toilet with no running water

If you have practiced the squat procedure properly, the dirty water will all be in the toilet. Floor water is usually spilled from the water source to its destination. In other words, water on the floor in this situation does not necessarily imply that it is dirty.

Most squat toilets do not flush by the push of a handle but by the action of your pouring water into the toilet. It sometimes takes quite a bit of water to clean the toilet, and you, of course, want to leave the toilet ready for the next person.

Since the toilets are not flushed with any kind of water pressure or force, toilet paper will quickly cause a clogging problem. So if you must use toilet paper you simply must not put it in the toilet. You will have to place the paper in a plastic bag and dispose of it in a proper place or burn it.

Right — or left?

And now for the final problem in facing a real squat toilet — how to stand on it. Which way do the feet go?

Which way is sometimes the subject of tourist jokes by locals because tourists tend to squat in the wrong direction. Many locals believe you should place your rear over the drain hole in the toilet. The drain hole is usually toward the back of the toilet bowl in ceramic toilets.

Non-ceramic toilets frequently have holes in the middle and no foot pads. In the case of the latter, do as you wish as long as you use the hole. Some feel that the shallow end of the toilet is better for preventing splashes. You will have to discover from experience which way you prefer to squat.

To add to the confusion, the space in which the toilet is sometimes enclosed can be so small that it will be comfortable only for children. Turning around once over the toilet in this small space is too risky for your feet.

Backing in can be equally dangerous. So you may have to

endure some snickers from the locals if you face the wrong way.

All this business of squatting and using water instead of toilet paper may seem terribly complicated and require acrobatic abilities. But after a few practice sessions, you will be amazed at how simple it all is.

Remember that many years ago it took months for you to learn how to use a western toilet. If you have forgotten, be assured your mother remembers.

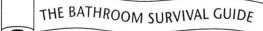
SQUAT TOILETS: Unplugging the mystery

Chinese village squat toilet trench:
Observing proper etiquette is necessary

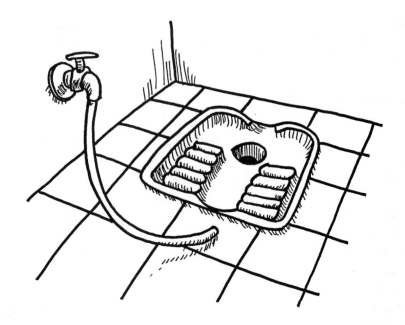

Squat toilet in Egyptian Oasis home, where running water is available.
To use, a traveler squats atop the corrugated footsteps, with posterior
elevated over the hole. Running water from the hose is used
for cleaning oneself and for flushing the toilet.

My own first encounter with an unfamiliar toilet was in
Turkey, when I saw my first squat toilet. What a
mystery! How do you manage? It seemed apparent from
the faucet and pitcher next to the toilet that water was
involved, but how was it used? Since there was no handle
for flushing, what did you do?

I was much too embarrassed to ask a local person and even
too embarrassed to mention the problem to my traveling
companions. They, knowing no more than I, never alluded
to the problem. So we muddled through, so to speak.

When I used toilet paper, I was chagrined to find the toilet
was clogged on the next visit. Since it appeared that my
use of paper was causing the problem, sometimes I'd
throw water at my private parts, hoping for the best and

thoroughly wetting my clothing. But nothing seemed to work! And I very likely left behind a path of clogged toilets and distressed toilet owners.

It was not until a few years later in India that the mystery of squat toilets was solved for me. After a thirty-five hour airplane ride, my friend and I arrived in Bangalore with a good case of jet lag and exhaustion. Our gracious Indian hosts showed us to our room and bath.

Waiting for us in the bathroom was a half-and-half toilet (pictured on page 50). I ventured to try it first. Sitting was too uncomfortable for me because there is no seat and the facility was too high for my feet to touch the ground. Amazingly, it seemed apparent to me that my standing on the "feet part" of the toilet and squatting would be more appropriate.

My shoes, with their slippery soles, allowed one of my feet to slide into the toilet. When I came out of the toilet with a soggy foot, my friend screamed with laughter.

Lotas containing water are used in Pakistan for indoor toilets. To use, tip the spout toward area to be cleansed.

Her turn was to come. My friend emerged from the same toilet mumbling that she needed to practice her aim as she dried her feet.

Our hysterics caused our host to inquire the next morning if we were having a problem. I think that since he had entertained Americans before, he suspected the truth. He was so concerned and kind we confessed our errors and ignorance. He explained all; the remainder of our six weeks' visit was spent in complete confidence. We had overcome the major obstacle to a happy stay in the real India. In fact, we came to like using squat toilets and to use water for cleansing afterward.

What is the attraction? One well-traveled leader of adventure tours summed up his feelings this way: The beauty of squatting is that your anatomy never has to touch places where many other anatomies have traveled.

On safari when nature calls

While on an early morning animal-viewing adventure in East Africa, nature may call and the guide will carefully search the landscape with his binoculars — for hungry lions. It is only after the area is secure from danger that the guide will release the passengers from the truck, with women to one side and men to the other.

Now what to do? Obviously, surrounded by such natural beauty, you are reluctant to pollute the landscape. You do not want to see young lions romping about in toilet paper.

The first step is to find some soft soil. If no shovel is available, dig a hole with the heel of your boot (people on safari usually wear boots or other sturdy footwear).

Creating toilet hole with boot

Squat and use the hole! Now, using the heel of your boot, kick the loose soil back over the hole until it's covered. If a rock is available, you can further secure the hole by placing a rock over it.

Boot covering used toilet hole

In some areas, this procedure is called digging a "cat hole." And don't leave behind any "paper flowers."

If you are in a desert region, or if the soil is too hard to dig, some people dispose of the toilet paper by bagging or burning. Since there is little rain in deserts, paper will not decompose for decades. Do we really want someone to have to deal with our dirty paper twenty years from now?

Note that using these holes in high winds is perilous. Be sure your feet are upwind of your rear.

On safari we spent our first night in the isolated western corridor of the Serengeti. As we sat around a roaring campfire, our guide warned us that if we did not want to become dinner for one of those magnificent animals we came to see, we were never to go beyond the perimeter of our camp, day or night. Right! We were not at the zoo.

If we needed a toilet in the night, we must first search the area with our flashlights from the safety of our tent. The light will reflect off an animal's eyes in the dark. If we saw no reflections, we could proceed, but no further than the back of the tent. Remember, the bushes were our toilets already.

With these fearful facts in my head, I went to bed. At home I never have the call of nature at night. But not an hour after going to bed in my tent, I had an urgent need. Just as I was gathering my courage to do something about it, there was snuffling outside the tent. Yes, a lion!

The next hour was agonizing. It appeared the visitor was only passing through but was taking its time. When it seemed safe, I unzipped the tent door just enough to put one foot and my rear out and did what I was so desperate to do — and jumped back in.

The next morning, as I carefully exited my tent, I saw that there were little toilet paper mounds just outside the door of each tent. Every morning thereafter, there also was an early morning cleanup crew.

At the end of the trip, we learned that our guide and African cooks always slept with just the screen door of their tents zipped. Despite the cold they had not zipped up the cloth door of the tent so they could always survey our tents and rush to our rescue if needed.

We were confronted by a different problem on an East African safari in a very populated country, Rwanda. Unable to find a vacancy in a campground, we drove on and on in the hope of finding some open ground suitable for camping. There was none. Every inch of land was either cultivated or inhabited. Finally, as dusk set in, we found an unoccupied gravel pit and moved in.

Any hope that we were in an uninhabited area was quickly dispelled when we were encircled by locals who were vastly entertained by our camp antics. We all smiled at each other, and occasionally the locals would offer a helping hand with our tents. This cultural exchange was quite delightful until toilet time.

On safari, bushes had been our toilet sites. But in a gravel pit there were neither bushes nor privacy.

We hit upon the plan of some of us creating a diversion while the others sneaked away in the gathering gloom toward mounds of gravel to find as much privacy as possible. But the local little ones were too sharp for these tactics and followed us. We decided we'd just have to put up with them.

A west African village pit-type public toilet. A large hole is covered with branches leaving a five-inch hole in the middle. The branches are then covered with whitewash. It was spotlessly clean. There is no door to the opening in the six-foot wall.

It was in Western Africa that I prayed for good aim. In a gleamingly clean village I was escorted to the equally spotless outhouse with its squat toilet. There was no water available here. This was the public toilet used by the entire village.

The toilet was a five-inch hole surrounded by a white-washed adobe ground and enclosed by a six-foot wall. I was horrified! Would my aim be good enough for this five-inch hole? I felt the reputation of all foreigners lay in my hands — or rear.

I was in desperate need. So, with full concentration, very slowly I relieved myself. It was a miracle. I left the toilet as I found it; the locals would not know the truth about aimless Americans. I did use toilet paper here as it was a pit toilet with no plumbing to clog.

Another friend reports the most scenic toilet she found in Africa was a squat toilet on the second stop up the Mt. Kilimanjaro trail.

It is located over a small waterfall and the toilet is open on the waterfall side so the water can be contemplated while you squat. Look for it when you climb Mt. Kilimanjaro. And do I have to suggest that you should not drink from this stream?

In 1994, I encountered a really primitive toilet in a desert village in Western India. A friend and I were attending a village marriage when we decided to explore the quaint village. We found a structure that was the proper size and in an appropriate place for a toilet. It was at the end of a desert garden. With curiosity we peered in and discovered no toilet whatever.

There was just ground and a small hole at ground level, not in the floor but in the back wall. The ground was clean. Our suspicions that this was a toilet were confirmed when two gracious village ladies rushed over to indicate that we were very welcome to use the facilities.

We declined since we had no idea what to do and the ladies spoke no English. There was no one there who could enlighten us. Fortunately, there are bushes even in the desert.

In Hong Kong, to my surprise, I discovered a similar toilet. After dining in a local noodle shop, I inquired for the facility. The manager was apologetic as he told me that the toilet might not meet my standards.

I told him I did not care as I was in desperate need. He showed me through the kitchen, where helpers were washing dishes with a hose connected to an outside faucet.

We stopped at a small room off the kitchen. It had only a cement floor and a hole in the back wall at ground level! He told me to use the floor as I must and the kitchen ladies would hose the floor.

After this adventure I was very thankful I had my usual gamma globulin shot, together with every other kind of shot that offered health protection.

Toilet bus

On a recent trip to Thailand I was visiting a large and imposing tourist attraction in a big city. Despite careful investigation I was unable to locate a toilet. It was necessary to ask.

Not speaking the language, I decided one of the guards who dealt often with tourists would understand "toilet" in English. Sure enough, the guard did seem to understand and indicated with waving hands that I was to go down the street and around the corner.

I followed his instructions but found the street around the corner to be lined with a tall wall and parked cars. I cruised the block — but no toilet. Again I asked a local, "toilet?" She indicated I was to return the way I had come. Again, nothing. My instinct was that these people were far too kind and generous to be playing a trick on a stupid tourist. I knew there had to be a toilet.

I returned to the ticket booth of the tourist attraction and asked again. This time they indicated the same direction, but said "bus." I repeated, Bus? They nodded. Ah, it was at a bus stop. I returned to the same block. Oh yes, there was a bus. I walked around it. No toilet.

But I noticed something odd about the bus. Against its front was a row of large potted plants, as if the bus wasn't going anyplace. The door of the bus was open — and what was that familiar odor? A toilet?

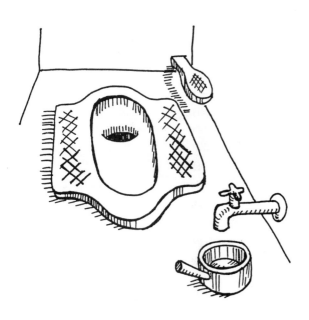

I hesitantly approached the open door and asked the attendant for the toilet. Yes, she said and motioned me in. Sure enough, it was a bus of only toilets. It was used by both sexes. There were small (very small) closed stalls in the middle and urinals in the rear.

Toilet bus stall

Each stall had its own water tap and a chemical flush squat toilet. In the front of the bus was a wash sink and a desk for the attendant. How ingenious.

In Egypt, across the river from Luxor in the Valley of the Kings, I discovered that movable toilets also seemed to be in fashion. At convenient locations around the tombs were parked trailer toilets. They had been deposited by a truck.

Each had a section for men and for women, with two stalls in each section. In the stalls were western toilets that flushed.

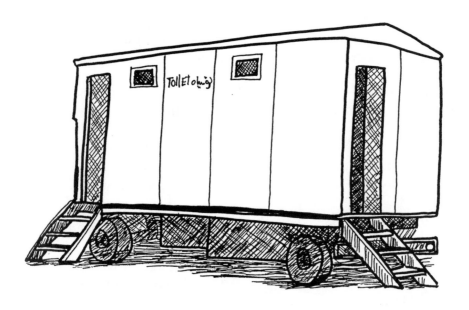

Valley of the Kings truck trailer toilet

Foreign trains also have squat toilets. Toilet doors are frequently locked in the station because trains usually have no holding tanks and the effluence goes directly on the tracks.

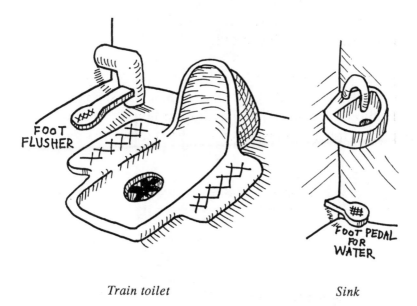

Train toilet   *Sink*

Ladies, when the trains move at high speed, you will find
high heels treacherous while using these toilets.

In Japan, trains have toilets that are used by both men
and women. Tourists will find the facilities' three-foot
by four-foot size small, but not the least of their problems.

The toilet hole is on a shelf about two feet above the floor,
with grab bars on each wall. It's low enough for men to
use as they stand on the floor, but women need to climb up
to squat, using the bars. Quite often, the shelf is very wet
and slippery.

At the Imperial Palace in Tokyo, the toilet is a
five-foot-square room with a four-sided floor that
slants downward toward the center. In the middle is a hole
with two footpads, one on each side. Upon exiting the
toilet, the user pulls a chain that releases a torrent of water
to flood the area. Beware of high water!

A Thai toilet arises in a lovely tropical setting next to a canal. It is a pit type with a large ceramic jar below to collect the waste.

After a delicious lunch of pork vindaloo in Goa, India, a traveler sought and found very clean stalls of squat toilets nearby. They were so spotless he was reluctant to use them.

But use them he must. He readied himself and as he was about to squat, to his horror, a pig's snout appeared in the toilet hole's opening. It seems the toilet's drain was a cement chute that ran to the ground in back of the facility, and pigs disposed of the refuse. This pig had become overly anxious.

As he exited, the traveler thought again about his lunch of pork vindaloo.

I encountered a squat toilet that is still a mystery to me. We were in Bhutan, a small Himalayan country, to witness a colorful Buddhist festival in a small village dominated by a monastery. While we watched the dancing, we were given numerous cups of tea by the locals. It wasn't long before the need for a toilet occurred.

The Bhutanese Monastery toilet in a small room attached to the upper floor of the monastery and cantilevered from the building. The human waste drops down the side of the monastery to the ground.

When we indicated our need, we were politely escorted into the monastery by a young monk. Since the toilet was on the second floor, we had to climb the typical Bhutanese stairs — a feat in itself. The stairs are thin strips of wood nailed to a large wooden platform. The platform leans against the opening of the floor above. With full bladder, I learned that one goes up these stairs sideways as the steep steps will accommodate only part of the side of your foot.

At the second floor, we were shown a small room cantilevered from the building. In its middle was a large carved object shaped like an old-fashioned toaster, but much larger. It was about two feet long and twenty inches high and was used by the monks as a toilet. It was very clean.

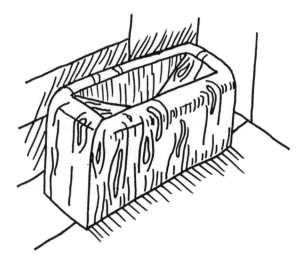

Bhutanese Monastery Toilet

But questions remained: Did you straddle it? Sit on it? We had no idea, and in our urgent state, we established it was beyond our abilities to figure it out.

The mystery of how exactly to use the Bhutanese Monastery Toilet remains: we decided on the more reliable bushes in the fields outside.

Travelers will discover other unusual toilets in Bhutan. Most of the houses are substantial two-story stone structures, the ground floor for animals and the upper for people. Pigs and chickens are the common barnyard creatures.

In each house, there is usually a small room with a hole in

the floor that opens directly into the ground floor. This is the toilet. The animals below dispose of the waste.

One Bhutanese public toilet I saw was a two-sided straw-walled structure in front of a small stream. Users straddle the stream out of sight of those traveling the road next to it.

Sometimes the locals of an area will do what is practical for them for toilet facilities. A friend on a recent visit to a rural area in the Soviet Union (or whatever it is now called) was shown wonderful and generous hospitality by a family in their new and fairly modern home.

After the hospitality, a familiar urge called. She was taken out the back door to a small building. One side of the building was the kitchen and the other side was an empty room containing only for a bucket.

Yes, this was IT. And it had already been used.

In China, parents have a unique way of dealing with small children, not yet toilet trained. The children wear long pants, but the rear seam is not sewn together.

When they squat, which seems to be natural for small children, the rear of the pants separates. Voila! NO dirty clothes.

In cities, squatting children can create a hazard. The City of Shanghai has dealt with the problem in downtown areas by creating small gratings on sidewalks, open to the sewers below.

There are two to a block and parents are urged to curb their children over these grates.

Chinese community toilet

If you visit China, don't expect western-style flush toilets in most areas. Not many homes have toilets of any kind. However, there are large public toilets for each neighborhood.

The communal toilet I visited was in a large concrete building. It consisted of a trench two feet deep running down the long side of the room. Every half hour, water was released into the trench to clean it out.

There were low partitions at intervals. The idea is to straddle the trench and squat.

A friend had to visit a Chinese community toilet for the first time after dining in a fancy restaurant. Much to her amazement, she had found that there was no toilet in the elegant restaurant. She was directed to follow a path to the local community toilet.

As she crossed a field, she found, from the distinctive odor, what was obviously the toilet. There were no written signs, as after all, the locals all know where the toilet is; they visit it daily.

She entered and was stunned. It was full of men, all squatting over the customary trench, holding newspapers in front of them to read. Not one even looked up.

She breathlessly backed out.

With embarrassment, a Chinese guide rushed to direct her to the women's side of the toilet — where she squatted over the trench and proceeded to do what she needed. She also noted that those people who brought newspapers recycled them in a very practical way.

Her travel group sometimes had difficulty finding toilets. Once they were forced to seek toilets in a grammar school, feeling certain there would be facilities large enough for a group. With considerable relief, they located what they were looking for.

As everyone positioned themselves in their awkward and unpracticed squats over the trench-type toilet, there was a school break and youngsters flooded into the toilet. They stopped abruptly and gaped with open mouths and wide eyes.

What a sight it must have been to see all these adult foreigners —complete with cameras dangling from necks — balancing precariously over the toilets.

These days, China is in the midst of change. Government ministries are in the process of building one thousand public "super toilets" in major cities.

The toilets are to be manned by attendants and equipped with mirrors, wash basins, doors on the stalls — and even toilet paper!

It was in Sumatra that a friend reached her limit — at least as far as usable toilets are concerned.

She's a world traveler who is no longer content with exploring well-traveled tourist paths. Traveling alone, she seeks more excitement and usually finds it in the outreaches of civilization.

After 25 years of travel, I was amazed that she had a difficult time recalling a single toilet story for me. I found that she could be so completely adjusted to strange environments that she doesn't pay any special attention to local toilets.

Usually.

But she was able to share one memorable toilet incident. It began during a twenty-six hour bus ride in Sumatra. When the bus stopped along the route, all passengers headed for the relief of the local public bath house. And so did my friend.

For women, the toilet was simply a rectangular room with a slightly tilted concrete floor. Women squatted on the floor, did their business, and then washed themselves from a large vat. My friend saw that the floor had become filled with a watery mess, which ran over everyone's feet.

Women washed themselves by throwing pans of water over their bottoms; they did not touch themselves or use paper. For practical reasons some local women wore no underwear.

For my friend, this was not a sanitary situation and one to be avoided. She told me that in this instance she backed away and found that a nice clump of bushes was a better choice of toilet for her.

In Egypt, in the Oasis of Kharga, is a well preserved Christian Necropolis. Here are 250 tombs of mud brick, some with early Christian paintings. You may wonder why such old buildings of mud are still standing, and the answer is that there is almost no rain in the Egyptian Western Desert and Upper Egypt (Luxor and Aswan).

The public toilet was a mud brick hut with a floor of hardened mud. The toilet could truly be called a hole in the ground. The toilet's opening was created by the middle half of a ceramic jug, about eight inches wide and narrowing to about five inches. It opened into a trench that emptied at the back of the hut. A touch of elegance was added by four large tiles surrounding the hole. Next to it was a plastic bottle holding water, an old tin can to use for washing, and a mound of ashes to be brushed over bowel movements.

The desert is so dry that human waste is not a problem. It dries in ten minutes or less and can then be brushed out the back of the trench.

Toilet at Necropolis in Kharga

Another little-visited sight in Kharga Oasis is the charming ruins of the Temple of Hibis (built by Darius I in 522 B.C.). The toilet is also a hole in the ground but, surprisingly, is made solely of clay and formed to look like a porcelain squat toilet. Though it appeared to be a little worn, the clay facility seemed to stand up to its job in this ultra-dry climate.

Mud brick hut for clay toilet   *Clay squat toilet*

The White Desert near the Farafra Oasis is among the most sterile deserts in the world. It is a daunting trip into this remote and isolated country. Of course, our toilet was the sand. Where we could find a secluded patch of sand, we used it.

Our Bedouin guides asked that we burn our toilet paper; otherwise, it would still be where we put it fifty years from now. But I found wet toilet paper is not easy to burn, even in this dry climate. So I simply put it in a plastic bag and burned it in the very hot bonfire at camp.

What? Squat toilets in the European Alps? Yes, flushing squat toilets are common in the hiking huts in the Alps of Switzerland, Austria and Italy. A friend encountered these while hiking. Toilet paper could be used in them, but was not provided.

She also encountered a squat toilet in France as she and her family had their first visit. After a delicious French dinner at a typical bistro in the heart of Paris, my friend was the first to visit the toilet. Much to her amazement, she was confronted with a small, square cubicle with a hole in the floor, with elevated ceramic footplaces. She had no difficulty figuring out how to use this squat toilet, though the position was decidedly awkward.

The water tank was located high on the wall with a chain pull to flush the toilet. But when she pulled the chain, the water rushed from the water tank with such force she had to leap out of the way — in fact, all the way out of the door to avoid getting drenched from the knees downward.

Fortunately, she had dressed herself completely before flushing. Needless to say, there was great hilarity when the rest of her party used the facility, but at least they'd been warned!

In the last several decades, San Francisco experienced a large influx of Asian immigrants who apparently were confounded by the strange and alien toilet facilities they encountered. The janitors at the San Francisco International Airport complained about shoe prints on toilet seats and broken seats, as well as used toilet paper and water on the floor.

It turned out that the refugees were simply practicing the polite toilet habits for squat toilets of their homelands. Once they learned about the proper use of the sit toilet, the immigrants quickly adjusted to American life.

Western tourists, in turn, often lack knowledge about the proper use of Asian (squat) toilets. You can imagine how disgusted the locals of an Asian country might be at our misuse of their facilities.

I encountered this problem in Thailand when I was seeking a toilet in a small village. I found the telltale tin shack and unlatched the door to find a lovely pink ceramic squat toilet imbedded in the dirt. Little plants were growing around it. There was a large pink plastic tub with water, no doubt from a well. It was on dirt, but was immaculate.

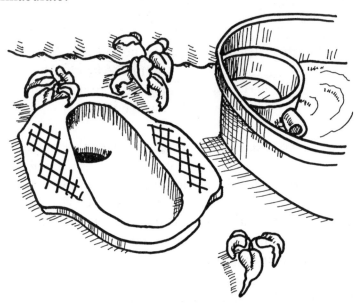

Thai squat toilet set in dirt, with handy tub of water

A local rushed up to tell me not to use this facility. He had obviously had experience with inexperienced foreigners befouling his clean toilet with toilet paper and other unspeakables. He directed me instead to use the nearby bushes.

TOILET

DOOR
LIFT TO PUT IN PLACE

Example of country squat outhouse

There are unexpected pleasures for city folk who hike into a village where there are no cars, electricity or running water. We had that pleasure when we hiked in southern Morocco to the village of Tirmtat. It sits in scenic, but very dry mountains.

We spent several days residing in a local home, where we slept on the roof, which was surrounded by an eight-foot wall with large window-like openings. It was quite private.

The toilet was a small room under the stairs that led to the roof. It had the usual squat toilet, which was flushed with water from a large can, which was carried in by hand from the town faucet. In the toilet hole, we found, was an empty plastic bottle. We soon determined that this was a good idea: in its position, the bottle acted as a sort of "stopper" to prevent odor and insects. You removed the bottle before using the squat toilet; once you were finished, you replaced it in the hole.

Village house in Tirmtat, Morocco.
Woman on right carries cans of water filled at town faucet.

Inside view of toilet. The empty water bottle in the center of the squat toilet prevents odors and insects and is removed for toilet use. There is a candle for light at night.

We encountered yet another unusual squat toilet next to the stepping stone trail to the Youth Hostel atop Mt. Davis on Hong Kong Island.

In a cement building were five stalls separated by two-foot-high walls. In each stall was a rectangular plastic pan with disinfectant in the bottom. When and where these pans were emptied was not clear.

We counted ourselves as fortunate that at the time we viewed them they had not been used. It was obvious that this toilet was to be used by both sexes.

In Morocco we discovered some surprising changes in squat toilets. It all began in Ouarzazate, Morocco, a tourist town on the edge of the Sahara desert, when we found that the costs of tourist hotels were beyond our budget.

So we were happy to discover a sparkling new hotel that we could afford. It was built for use by Moroccans. Each room had its own bathroom, which appeared to have the usual squat toilet, with a faucet and water container next to the toilet. On the wall behind the toilet was a lever. We experimented by pushing the lever and to our surprise, water came rushing into the toilet bowl. A flushing squat toilet!

There was no holding tank for water. The lever apparently works as a handle on a faucet. Ouarzazate is a prosperous town as a result of tourist money; the city has acquired a modern sewer system which can accommodate flushing toilets.

Actually, I had used flush squat toilets in Japan in 1979, but these toilets are a new development in developing countries.

For those who simply must have a squat toilet in their homes, it is now possible to achieve this goal. Some health stores offer a wooden structure that will convert a sit toilet into a squat toilet. It seems that squatting is recommended by some as the preferred position for people with hemorrhoid and constipation problems.

To convert your sit toilet to a squat toilet, you merely lift the existing toilet seat. Push the wooden squat toilet's structure around the sit toilet. You use a handy step to reach the top of the squat toilet. You then can turn around, place your feet on the wide part of the wooden structure, and do your business — squatting.

At left is a wooden squat toilet converter for a Western sit toilet. Now you can clamber atop your toilet to squat

SIT
TOILETS

Flushed with success
in the
Western world

Variations, challenges and other
novelties travelers may encounter

**Includes an introduction
to the marvels of the
B I D E T
and how to use it**

The Western sit toilet in all its glory

It's not clear when the act of sitting for a natural function began, but the Western world has accepted it as the proper method for waste elimination. Most of us in this country are accustomed to the modern ceramic sit toilet.

Sit toilets are found in the Western world and in some hotels in countries where squat toilets are more common. However, travelers should be aware that these toilets may differ in small respects. The local plumbers may be unfamiliar with proper installation; maintenance of Western toilets and replacement parts may be unavailable. There may be broken or missing toilet seats. For example, in 1995 in the International Airport in Casablanca, Morocco, there were no toilet seats on the sit toilets in the women's restroom. So we simply resorted to squatting over the sit toilet.

Sometimes, these toilets don't flush very well and require the pouring of water from a container to clean them. Proper flushing of toilets requires a great volume of water, and many countries simply don't have that much water pressure, water available, or even an adequate sewage system to handle the discharge. The problem with this type of flush toilet is that it will not accommodate toilet paper.

That was the case while I was living in Guatemala. To use the toilet, you placed your used toilet paper in a trash can next to the toilet — and then the toilet could be successfully flushed. In 1996, on my second trip to Egypt, I found that toilet paper was a disaster for most of the toilets we encountered. They would not flush; water overflowed.

As a guideline to head off potential disaster, travelers should note whether there is a large basket provided near the toilet. This is an indication toilet paper should not be put in the toilet. If the situation is not clear, ask. You, of course, do not want to create an international incident with overflowing or clogged toilets.

Sometimes you don't know quite what to do as you encounter various types of flushing sit toilets. The mystery toilet to the right was found in Guatemala.

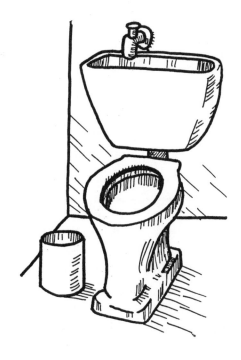

Encounter with Guatemalan mystery toilet: How do you flush it?

Note there is no handle for flushing. If you were to peer inside you'd see that the tank has absolutely no internal parts. However, there is a water faucet opening into the toilet water tank. The toilet is flushed by turning on the faucet for as long as necessary to adequately flush the toilet bowl. Unfortunately, in this case, I found that the faucet did not work.

But what an ingenious design! There is no need for endless repairs of valves, rods and other annoying parts usually found in toilet water tanks. Of course, the downside is that it takes longer to adequately flush the toilet, as there is not the volume of a full water tank to rush through the toilet bowel all at once. Note there is a container next to the toilet for used toilet paper.

I was reminded by a traveling friend that we had encountered a similar toilet in 1970 in Spain. Our pensione had a toilet that had no familiar flushing mechanism. We were puzzled. The mystery was solved when my friend washed her hands in the sink. We discovered that the sink drain was connected to the toilet. Away it flushed! An excellent way to conserve water in drought-ridden areas!

One of the most common types of sit toilets is the outhouse, both in the United States and throughout various parts of the world. Sit-type outhouses were fairly common in urban and rural areas until comparatively recent times. In some parts of the world, they remain the only way to go.

As a child in the 1940s I spent my summers at a camp in the country. I adored the camp experience and looked forward to summer. However, because I was a city girl raised with Victorian attitudes and sensibilities, I found that my summer delights were jolted by my encounters with the camp's primitive outhouse.

The pit-type outhouse consisted of three stalls in one building at some distance from our cabins. Only the most urgent need would force me, gagging, into one of these, not just because of modesty but the smell and flies. I was just not accustomed to the outhouse.

A modern, well-ventilated outhouse

But during this same period of time, I had an uncle who lived in a small Southern village and had modern facilities in his home. He steadfastly refused to use the indoor facilities and continued to trek to his outhouse at the back of his garden. He not only preferred the out-of-doors but firmly believed indoor facilities were unsanitary.

A good friend who grew up in Costa Rica said his village got indoor plumbing in the 1950s. Everyone in the village resisted this move indoors until they were forced into it; all outhouses were destroyed by the government. Curiously, he cannot recall any distaste for the outhouse. Others who used outdoor facilities also have reported no adverse feelings about them.

There are, it seems, hazards to pit-type outhouses. A friend who grew up in the country attended a rural church that had no running water. A pit outhouse was all that was available to the congregation. After services one Sunday the ladies lined up in front of the outhouse. One of the larger members of the congregation entered the structure. Sounds of crashing wood, screams and a splash shortly followed. The wooden floor had rotted and could not bear the weight of this unfortunate lady. She was saved, but need I describe the scene further? Perhaps it is wise to check wooden floors on older outhouses before entering.

A real hazard of pit toilets is the possibility of dropping valuables such as car keys into the waste pit of the toilet. They will be virtually irretrievable. I suggest you leave such items a safe distance from the toilet hole. And when you are finished, close the lid of the toilet to discourage bugs and odors.

Not all outhouse toilets are of the pit variety. In a California park I found a modern outhouse with a flush toilet. The outhouse was formed of plastic and had a metal floor. The flushing pedal was to the left of the toilet. But not all the wrinkles are out of this modern outhouse: I weigh 115 pounds, but I had to stand on the pedal firmly with both feet to be able to flush the toilet.

Modern California outhouse toilet
with flushing capabilities:
A little too firm for the author's tastes

Historic sight: *A unique two-story outhouse from the 1800s, still standing (though not in use) at the Union Hotel, San Juan Bautista, California. In this unusual design, there is one outhouse on the top story and two on the lower. The upper toilet was reached by a catwalk from the hotel's second floor. The two-story outhouse concept never grew in popularity, possibly because occupants of the lower outhouses grew concerned that the top outhouse might spring leaks.*

Outhouses of the pit type are still found in rural public parks, at summer cabins, and in some rural areas. A well-ventilated and maintained outhouse can be pleasant to use. Proper etiquette requires that you distribute a little soil, if available in a nearby box, on your eliminations. Lower the lid on the toilet before you leave to prevent odors and flying insects. Try to leave the facility reasonably neat and clean for those who follow.

Travelers to various parts of the world may feel only momentary relief as they find a sit toilet instead of a squat toilet. For example, in outward appearances our hotel in western China was modern and promised western-style facilities. The reality was that my room's toilet ran continuously but didn't really flush. I found that only one toilet worked in the entire floor of eight rooms. In the spirit of tourist camaraderie, the occupants of that toilet generously shared their facility.

On a visit to one of the established romantic spots of the world, Bali, I had the experience of a romantic bathroom. Attached to our detached bungalow was a modern western bathroom; but looking up, I noticed one unusual thing about it: no roof! Sunshine streamed in. Colorful tropical plants dangled over the wall. While bathing under the sun or stars, I came to love the sense of being out-of-doors.

Coping with Bali's open air toilet

Because of Bali's tropical climate, it was all quite charming. Alas, not all was perfect. I innocently left the toilet seat down (there was no cover) and went away for the day. When I returned, I sprinted for the toilet but immediately arose. The seat was burning hot from the equatorial sun. Morning brought another problem to our open-air paradise — a rain storm. When was the last time you used an umbrella for your morning constitutional?

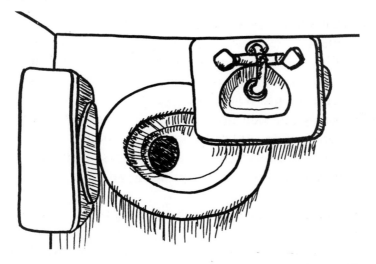

Contortionist's delight: Sink overhangs commode aboard vessel

On the Nile River, I was traveling from Luxor to Aswan on a twelve-cabin African Queen-type boat. Definitely not one of the usual tourist ships (called "gin palaces" by locals), our small vessel had three communal toilets — each one different.

The one I most enjoyed was crammed into the space of a small closet. When I entered, I realized that the boat builder had a problem, and, for that matter, so did I. In order to get a small sink in the room, toilet space had been sacrificed. The sink was half over the toilet. I solved my problem by sitting on the toilet with my upper body leaning at a sharp angle and with one elbow in the sink.

In India, after a week of camping in the desert with no water for bathing, we arrived at a brand-new tourist resort on the edge of the desert town of Bhuj. There were lovely new huts complete with a bathroom with sit toilets and showers. Lucky us! We rushed to use these facilities only to discover there was no water. The water delivery of the day had not yet arrived. But we found that the resort was located on a large reservoir that held the town's water, so we hired some local lads to carry water from the reservoir to flush our toilets.

The toilet appeared to be a modern sit toilet. But looking closer, we saw that the toilet's water tank extended a few inches over the toilet opening. The lid rested on your back when you sat on the toilet, causing you to crouch forward. The simple solution was to remove the toilet lid.

In some countries, tourist facilities attempt to accommodate all possible toilet habits by using what I refer to as a half-and-half toilet: half sit and half squat.

The toilet is one to two feet above the floor. The area where you sit also has foot rests. You can sit on it somewhat uncomfortably or stand on it somewhat hazardously.

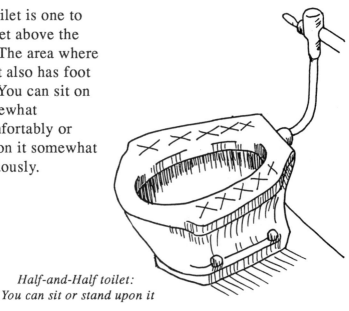

Half-and-Half toilet:
You can sit or stand upon it

TOILET SEAT

TOILET
PAPER
CONTAINER

Combination sit-and-squat Thai toilet: Bridging the gap?

Thai public toilets are also sometimes adjusted to accommodate habits of both Westerners and Asians, with varying degrees of success. The facility above started out as a bright pink Western sit-type toilet.

Note that the toilet seat can be removed so that those desiring to do so can precariously squat on the porcelain rim. Or, by replacing the toilet seat, you can use it as a standard sit-type toilet. The toilet flushing lever remains, but beware: It is for show only. To flush the toilet, you must dip water from the tank next to the facility and pour it into the toilet.

Don't throw used toilet paper into the toilet bowl, for it will not flush away. Instead, place your used toilet tissue into the receptacle next to the toilet.

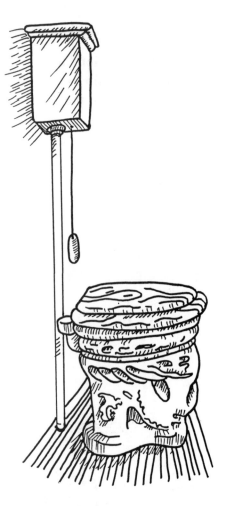

European flush toilet: Gravity can provide lots of water pressure

Be prepared to encounter some old- fashioned toilets still in use in Europe. The water tank is close to the ceiling so that gravity helps flush the water through the toilet, usually with some force, when a chain is pulled. The water runs from the back of the toilet toward the front. Unlike Western flush toilets with their large bowls of water, the organic deposit goes into a small depression in the toilet bowl, which contains a small amount of water. Flushing pushes the deposit forward into the waste pipe. These old toilets are the official water closet, known as the W.C. The ornate water closet pictured here is from turn-of-the- century Great Britain and is still in use.

Have you ever been attacked by your bowel movement? Yes, actually chased! A friend experienced this event in his apartment in Moscow.

He had noticed his toilet, although outwardly appearing to be an old but normal closet-type Western-style toilet, had two internal differences. The drain hole was in the front part of the toilet bowl instead of the rear, and at the rear of the bowl was a slight spoon-shaped depression.

The surprising event occurred the first time my friend had a major movement in the toilet. He pulled the chain to flush the toilet and turned to leave. Splat! Right on the back of his legs.

Later, experimenting with his toilet, he learned the force of the water from the water tank high above the toilet propelled the excrement across the large spoon-shaped depression and over the rim of the toilet, especially when the seat was up. What a puzzling way to construct a toilet.

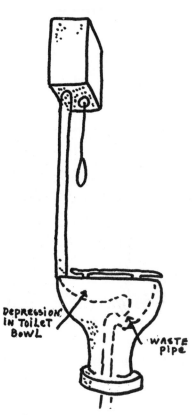

But why? A Russian friend helpfully explained that this toilet design was developed in the late 1800s, supposedly so that the depression could collect excrement for easy removal to the Russian fields for use as "night soil" fertilizer. The sole purpose of the water flush, the friend reported, was to rinse and clean the bowl after the excrement was manually removed.

Anatomy of spitting Russian toilet

Tall story or not, my friend in Moscow devised a way to deal manually with the spitting toilet, but how I will not reveal. I leave it to imaginative readers to ponder how they would solve my Moscow friend's toilet problem.

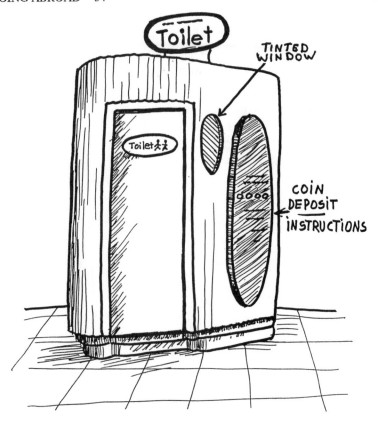

Modernistic London public street toilet

Some of the latest developments in European toilets can be rather daunting experiences for the uninitiated. I'm referring to the new public pay toilets: futuristic in appearance, made of molded plastic, located on city streets. The toilets are for use by both sexes.

You drop a coin in a slot and the door opens to reveal a glistening molded plastic toilet with a fragrant air. It is very clean; once you are inside, the door will slide closed and lock. While you do your business, there is even music to listen to.

After you depart, the facility is completely cleaned by automation. The ledge holding the toilet bowl (which has no outlet and is the size of half a basketball) tilts by pneumatic lifts and drains the toilet. The ledge and toilet are thoroughly flushed, washed and disinfected.

There are warnings to be observed. On the outside of the toilet structure, you are told the following information:

> *After each use of this heated cubicle, the floor and seat are automatically cleaned and disinfected. Children under 10 must be accompanied.*

When you leave, you are advised not to leave parcels inside. Obviously, not unless you also want them washed and disinfected.

Though I have used this facility with success, I still sometimes worry. Would the automatic washing process begin if you accidentally opened the door and closed it without leaving? Say you asked your friend standing outside to pass you a needed item through the open door and then you closed it? If somehow you were caught in all this automation, would you emerge wet, glistening — and also disinfected?

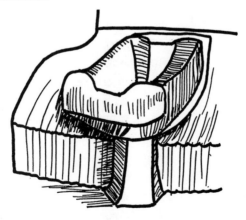

Modernistic street toilet's gleaming throne

There are other unusual approaches to public hygienic toilets. One friend spotted a different sort of toilet in the French Village of Redon in a pizza parlor. After using the toilet, she pushed a button which started a mechanism that, in addition to flushing the toilet, rotated the round toilet seat horizontally. The part of the seat just used rotated out of sight and a new section, which had been disinfected, appeared for use by the next patron.

Another hygienic concept is the Hygolet, a Swiss developed plastic-swathed toilet seat. For each use, a public toilet seat is encased with an individual sanitary plastic sleeve. A button is pushed to transfer the used plastic to a separate chamber and to unreel a clean new plastic sheath.

The idea is to provide a really sanitary and clean toilet seat and, at the same time, eliminate disposable seat covers which can clog plumbing. It also saves travelers from having to fashion makeshift seat covers of toilet paper. No longer needed is the mid-air hovering that many women adopt when confronted with a public toilet, which only adds to the wet seat problem.

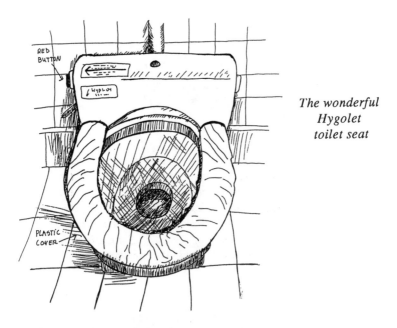

The wonderful Hygolet toilet seat

In Europe and sometimes in Latin America, you may be confronted by a bidet. For the uninitiated, they are not urinals, toilets or for washing the feet. They resemble a Western toilet in shape and material (ceramic) but the inside is quite different. There is a spigot, or water outlet, which projects water upward in a steady stream.

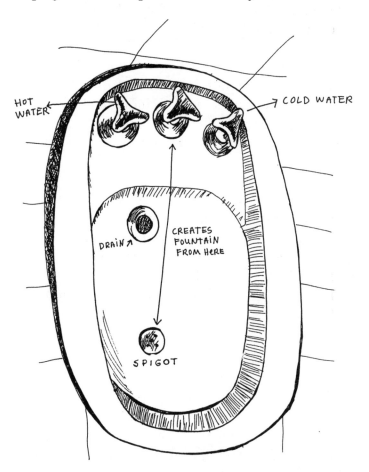

HOT WATER

COLD WATER

DRAIN

CREATES FOUNTAIN FROM HERE

SPIGOT

Inside view of bidet: When only the hot or cold water faucets (outer knobs at top) are turned on, the water circulates from under the rim of the bowl to flush the bidet. By adjusting the center faucet (see arrow in illustration), you can create a fountain of water of a temperature and a volume you desire for washing your private parts. The water rises from a spigot located in the bottom of the bowl. Some bidet designs use only two faucets to fill the bowl for washing.

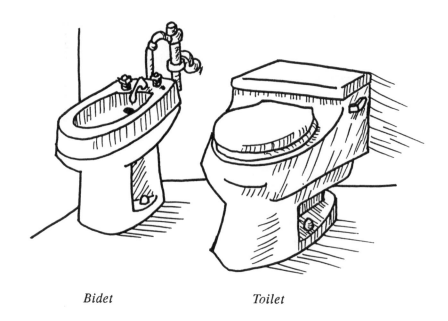

Bidet   *Toilet*

The bidet, usually found next to the toilet, is used from a crouch for rinsing the private parts of your body after toilet use. But bidets, it seems, are as puzzling to Americans as squat toilets.

For example, some years ago in France my neighbor encountered his first bidet. He had no idea what it was for and decided to use it as a vase (toilet-like admittedly) for roses. Decades later, on another encounter with bidets and still uncertain of their proper use, he decided he'd use the facility at last — for soaking his tired feet.

Sometimes bidets are too near the toilet. I encountered such a situation in a hotel in Marrakech, Morocco. The bidet faced the toilet, leaving just two inches between them.

I had to straddle the bidet in order to sit on the toilet.

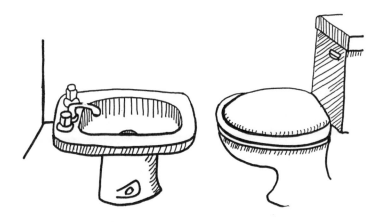

Bidet close to toilet   *Toilet*

Portable bidets can be found in Asian countries. They do not look like Western bidets but the purpose of cleaning the private body parts is the same.

The portable bidet usually consists of a hand-held water hose with sprayer on the end and a spigot on the wall to control the water flow. It will be in reach of the toilet and is used while sitting or squatting on the toilet.

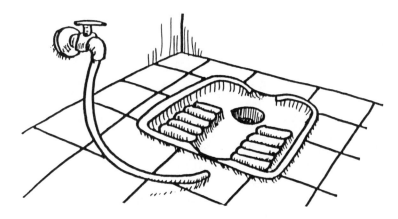

Portable bidet found in Asia: The hose is for cleaning oneself as well as flushing the toilet

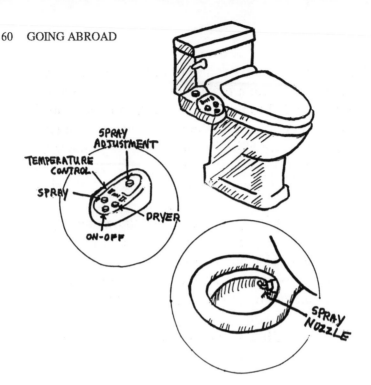

Japanese bidet and sit toilet: The ultimate combination?

Travelers in Japan may encounter the very latest combined bidet and sit toilet — advertised as the ultimate for personal hygiene.

A water nozzle is located in back of the toilet seat. A control box is next to the toilet to control the spray and nozzle. When the spray button is pressed, the water pressure extends the nozzle approximately two inches at a forty-three degree angle. Water gushes from the nozzle in a spray, which can be used for as long as necessary for cleaning. A ceramic heater warms the water. When the water is turned off, the nozzle retracts and the tip is automatically cleaned.

Press another button, and the spray of water is followed by a warm breeze for drying. This is certainly a hands-off approach to personal hygiene.

In Egypt we frequently found modern Western toilets that were equipped with a bidet. Since these bidets appeared to have been added to the toilet in an improvised fashion, they can hardly compare to the sophisticated Japanese toilet. Yet they were effective and did their job. They also kept the toilets flushing by eliminating the use of toilet paper, which many Egyptian toilets cannot handle.

One friend, after having mustered the courage to try a bidet wash, came to prefer their use to toilet paper. He discovered the device at a hotel in Luxor, Egypt, when he lifted the lid of his bathroom's standard porcelain toilet and saw the bidet's open mouth pointed straight up at his face. Fascinated by the plumbing, he bent down for a closer look. A flexible metal tube came from a wall faucet, snaked under the back of the seat, curved toward the water in the bowl and bent back up in a lazy "U" shape. Turning on the bidet's faucet, he watched as water gently sprang up as if from a drinking fountain.

He decided to try it. Squatting until he felt centered over the bidet spray, he opened the water faucet for a firm flushing. It was great, he reported: A refreshing experience in a hot dry climate. He now dreams of adding a bidet to his toilet at home.

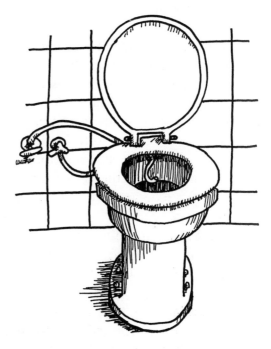

Egyptian improvised bidet toilet:
A flush that refreshes

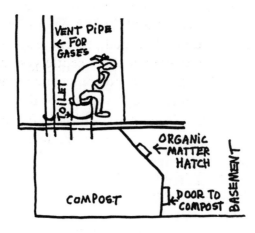

Swedish toilet for composting: All natural

For some time, the Swedish have been using a toilet to eliminate the sewage system and make practical use of the waste products. A similar toilet system is also available in this country. I recently inspected a modern composting toilet used by a couple living in the desert, where no water is available. They were thrilled with the composting toilet and felt everyone should use one. It was odorless, as they so proudly pointed out.

Composting Toilet:
Note that you
step up
to reach the
elevated throne

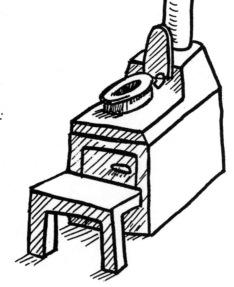

Their toilet was designed for a household of one to three people for year-round use. It took little more space than a regular toilet, provided one-hundred percent recycling, and used no electricity, water, chemicals or septic system. A four-inch pipe and the heat from the compost creates a chimney effect to draw air through and out of the system. There is no odor. Larger designs are available for use by more people, and these toilets require more space.

Even in the category of sit toilets, travelers sometimes encounter unique innovations.

Once, when I was in the airport ladies' room in Tallahassee, Florida, I could discover no means for flushing the toilet. I called out the problem to my aunt, who repeatedly told me to open the door. A rather strange answer, I thought. Finally, I followed her instruction and opened the door to the stall — the toilet flushed! Yes, the toilet flushes when the door to the stall is opened. No more encounters with unflushed toilets left by inconsiderate people.

Automatic flushing toilets seem to be appearing more frequently in public places. When there is no flushing handle, you can suspect the toilet will flush automatically. Some are designed to flush as soon as you arise from the toilet seat while others do not flush until you leave the stall. Some have a button on the top of the automatic device for extra flushing.

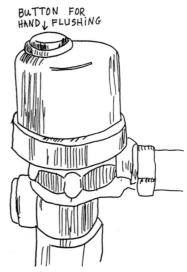

Automatic flushing device located at the back of toilet. This device has a button for hand flushing

Consider also the innovative world's highest public toilet atop Mount Everest, which long needed a decent public bathroom.

To get to the 20,000-foot elevation, Sherpas had to disassemble the toilet into seven parts and then lug them up by hand, including the 300-pound stainless-steel cubicle with its wood-seat toilet. Held in place by steel cables, the public toilet is promised to work (somehow) in high-altitude temperatures down to ten degrees Fahrenheit.

According to sketchy news reports, the toilet's first eager customer was a member of the British team studying the problem of disposal of mountain climbers' wastes.

A niggling question arises: Who is going to clean it?

Another innovation, of sorts: There's a possible solution to the seat-up, seat-down argument in the land of the sit toilet. It's called the Beep Seat, developed by a California inventor, and it consists of a small electronic device easily attached to any toilet seat.

It beeps when the seat has been left up.

THE BATHROOM SURVIVAL GUIDE

USEFUL
PRIVY
INFORMATION

**How to find a toilet abroad,
toilet etiquette, maintaining privacy
even when there isn't any — and
dealing with that old bugaboo
(or lack of it), toilet paper**

Public toilet in India: Doorless, for men only — and unmarked

How to find
a toilet abroad

Let's face it: Sometimes when you're abroad it's difficult to find a toilet. Public toilets are not common in most countries. Moreover, the toilets available to you may be very strange, sometimes with odd-looking fixtures, for one sex only, and in some cases, may not even have any doors.

Toilets abroad may not be identified by written word or graphic signs. This is especially true in countries where there are few tourists or where a part of the population is illiterate. After all, these facilities are used by the locals — and they know where they are, anyway. So why bother with a sign?

It may be comforting to travelers to know that I have traveled with friends for more than twenty-five years and almost never did any of us understand the languages of the countries we visited. But I have always been able to locate toilets. These are some shortcuts I take:

First of all, language is a problem if you don't speak it. I've also found that many handy foreign language phrase books fail to communicate properly on such an urgent and daily necessity as "Where is the toilet?"

The word, *toilet*, is what you want. Outside of the United States, asking for a "rest room" will result in locals' puzzled frowns. Requesting a "bathroom" probably will get you a bath but not a toilet. The word "toilet" is widely understood.

TOILET دورة ميــاه

Sign announcing Egyptian toilet

Since toilets abroad are not to be found on every street corner or in every building, where do you find them? In my own experience, I've found that the best, most reliable place to locate a toilet is at a restaurant. If there's a problem, ordering a drink or some food nearly always can get you access to a toilet.

Lobbies of first-class hotels are another good source, but be aware that sometimes these hotels have guards at the front door to keep out people who look like they don't belong. Toilets can also be located at tourist attractions.

If you are traveling on public transportation, at each stop, just follow the crowd. I do. The crowd will usually be headed for food or toilets.

In some countries public toilets are used by both sexes.
My first encounter with a unisex toilet was in a
restaurant in Morocco, and I can speak neither Arabic or
French. The waiter understood my gestures and my need
and pointed me to the toilet. As I started to open the door
to the toilet, a man came out.

Oops! But I could find no other toilet. I scurried back to
the waiter, and pointed at the facility with a horrified look
on my face. Grinning, he escorted me to the same toilet
and opened the door, indicating that I was to go in. Inside,
I found a large room with some stalls and a urinal. It was
used by both sexes at the same time. I quickly headed for a
stall, remembering Rule Number One for foreigners
abroad: If you don't find the toilet you want, be ready to
use the toilet you find.

If you don't speak the language, you can communicate
your needs by pantomime. I have found that pantomime
is the easiest and most effective language to use for
finding toilets. It will be obvious to the local person that
you cannot speak the language and no one will try to
explain anything to you because they know you won't
understand. You may even be taken by the hand and led to
your goal. Don't forget to smile your gratitude for any
help you receive.

Don't be shy about using pantomime. Let's say you find
yourself in a location where toilets might exist; so, you
rub your hands together in a washing motion and bring a
questioning look to your face (or a desperate look,
depending on your need.) I've found that you will
probably be directed to a hand-washing facility. Good —
the toilet will be nearby.

If you still can't find a toilet, return to your local helper
with a more desperate, questioning look on your face, and

use your hands rubbing your lower abdomen to emphasize
your needs. People throughout the world, I've found, are
usually sympathetic and quick to understand this universal
need. They will usually direct you to the toilet of your sex,
if there are separated toilets.

A final word on the subject: Since toilets available to
the public abroad are not abundant, and even though
your immediate need may not be great — I recommend
you use every toilet you find.

Etiquette

Every culture has its own etiquette in reference to toilet
and bathing habits. To avoid embarrassing misunder-
standings and misadventures, you should try to determine
what is considered proper at your destination.

Remember that many of our attitudes originated in
Victorian times when functions of the water closet were
considered a shameful secret. In our culture, we have
sufficient places for privacy, but this is not true everywhere. Just because privacy is scarce does not mean there
will not be toilet etiquette.

A traveling companion described a recent trip to Japan.
She had been informed that public facilities are
frequently used by both sexes, and she was simply to avert
her eyes when encountering the opposite sex and continue
about her business. This worked quite well, and she came
to accept the situation. But one day she rushed into a train
station toilet, carefully averted her eyes from the men
there, and went about her business. Imagine her surprise
when she left and discovered there was a ladies' room next
door — she had been using the men's room! But in polite
Japan, no one seemed to take notice of her error.

Though she was in the wrong place, she was doing the right thing. In cultures where privacy and toilet facilities are limited, the accepted etiquette is to avert the eyes. In other words, when you enter a facility in use or see a local person answering the call of nature in a field or roadside, don't stare. Keep in mind that to everyone around you that event simply is not occurring.

Privacy

Tourists who are accustomed to privacy sometimes have problems with the lack of it. Most places in the world have toilets, or, if they do not, at least have a place for some privacy when one feels the urge to be relieved. These may be the traveler's friends: a bush, a wall, or even a hilly mound.

But consider the privacy problems in a place where there is no escape: the ice of Antarctica. There are no trees, bushes, or hills, and everything you do is fully visible to everyone else in your party. Joe Murphy, author of the book *South to the Pole by Ski*, was part of a group of two women and nine men who were the first Americans to ski overland to the South Pole. For two months, as they crossed the continent, the author noted that everything they did was fully visible to everyone else in the party: one's toilet was a matter of public observation. The Antarctic darkness was no provider of cover either, for in the summer the sun shines twenty-four hours a day.

Joe says the only way to go about one's toilet was to wander a few hundred yards away from the group, place your back to the wind, and do your business — all in full observation. As time passed and the explorers grew weary of going out so far, the distance from the main party kept declining. In camp, however, the explorers carved a slit trench and strategically placed snowmobiles on either side.

They rigged a white canvas shield in front for privacy. Joe found that it was useful to use the makeshift toilet in the morning before the camp broke up for the day or to train yourself to use it after supper.

An acquaintance had a problem finding privacy when she and a friend visited relatives on a farm in Finland. When they reached the rural area, they indicated a need for a toilet and were quickly escorted from the house and through the barn to a small back room. Here they found a sit-down toilet of the pit variety, with three sit holes and no partitions. The relative, without hesitation, lifted her skirts and sat over one hole and indicated the other two for the girls' use. They were horrified, accustomed to privacy and puritanism. However, urgency required compliance. This adventure was the beginning of many tense and uncomfortable hours while they waited for their chance to visit the toilet without the entire family present.

In my experience there are a number of foreign toilets where there is no privacy available, and travelers will simply have to find ways to cope. One suggestion is to carry a newspaper. As you do your business you can become absorbed in reading your newspaper. Not only will you not notice your neighbors but it can be your "wall." And when you are finished, you can find a practical way to recycle it.

Strange as it may sound, you might also study the example of the cat. Cats love privacy in their toilet habits, but house felines are frequently forced into public exposure in their poorly positioned litter boxes. While in an embarrassing situation, cats assume a far-away, spaced-out look as if the feline were in another place altogether. A cat is a master of this. With a little practice, you can successfully imitate the cat. I do.

Expectations

People maintain toilet facilities that are clean by their culture's standards. They don't understand why foreigners sometimes cringe at what they see. Yet these same travelers abroad will, without hesitation, walk into their homes in street shoes. Some cultures consider shoes a greater source of filth than toilets. In some countries, a separate pair of slippers resides outside the toilet and is for use only in the facility.

You must also remember that local people have not been to your country and don't know what you want or are accustomed to. They have no frame of reference; your expectations, questions and demands may be confusing to them. Try to understand their way and accept it as valid and you will avoid unnecessary stress. Of one thing you can be certain: Things will not be like home. If that's truly what you want, you should consider staying home or going first class.

About Toilet Paper

To flush a toilet successfully requires a great deal of water — more than is available in many places — and an adequate sewage system. You should be aware that the use of toilet tissue designed for a Western-style flush toilet can be a menace in other toilet facilities.

What happens when toilet paper is put in a fixture that does not have enough water pressure to push it out of the toilet bowl? The first piece endlessly circles the bowl when the toilet is flushed. If you add a second piece, that only joins the first in its endless journey. Each additional piece only contributes to the problem; soon there is one giant blobby mess and the toilet is too repulsive to use. And it still hasn't flushed.

To solve the problem, baskets or cans are placed next to the toilets as a receptacle for *used* toilet paper. In Brazil, you'll even see signs asking that you do not place paper in the toilet, but in the baskets: "Favor nao jogar papel no vaso."

In some cases, local toilet paper is flimsy enough to disintegrate easily. That's so it can be used in local toilets, but beware: You'll often find it also seems to disintegrate in the hand, before it gets to the toilet.

In Europe be prepared for a tissue experience. The toilet paper you'll find in some flush toilets can be surprisingly different from what you are accustomed to use. I have heard descriptions of various European papers as sandpaper, butcher paper and even waxed paper. Some of it will scratch you, irritate you, or merely smear instead of clean you. For these reasons, you might prefer to carry a few sheets at a time on your person of your own favorite toilet tissue from home.

In Southeast Asia, where water is common to cleanse yourself in the squat toilets, imported rolls of toilet paper have found a different function. I was amazed the first time I saw these rolls displayed in lovely, colorful canisters on restaurant tables — to be used by diners as napkins.

Decorative, too!

Not all places use toilet paper. Some use newspapers or whatever is at hand for pit toilets. Peasants in the fields use leaves and sticks. Before you try this, be sure you know what kind of shrubbery you use because other countries have their equivalent of poison oak and poison ivy.

A Chinese friend who has returned to her homeland a number of times reports that in the countryside, the locals use a stick, resembling a Popsicle stick, in the same way we use toilet paper. If this seems strange, recall that our ancestors were fond of corn cobs.

Toilet Fees

In many countries public toilets are financed by users and would not exist without this support. Be prepared to pay a small fee to the attendant who maintains the facility.

Sometimes, communities resort to unusual ways of financing their facilities. One large monastery in Thailand keeps its toilets open through unusual local contributions. Over each stall of a row of toilets is inscribed the name of the donor.

Signs

Travelers may encounter unusual signs announcing a toilet.

Sign for a sit-type toilet

The sign on the left was found outside the door of a toilet in a modern restaurant in Southeast Asia. Inside, we found that the bathroom was complete with the latest western fixtures.

Remember, this is a country of squatters, but the sign makes it quite clear that here one sits.

A urinal for pregnant women? Oddly enough, I found the
next sign on the door of the men's room in Southeast Asia.

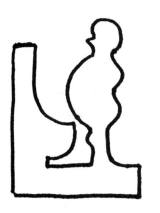

Who uses this — and how?

This was puzzling; we had to
ask. The answer we received
was that local modesty
forbids the showing of
genitals. This was simply a
sign showing that this men's
room has urinals.

Another sign, consisting of
two letters "WC," is also
fairly common. WC means
"water closet," which is what
Europeans sometimes call
the toilet. But the use of
initials, or abbreviations, can sometimes give rise to
confusion.

There's a story going around that a little old English
lady was looking for a room in a rural area of
Switzerland and wrote for help. She asked whether there
was a "W.C." in the house or nearby for her use. Not
understanding that she was asking about the toilet, the
rural Swiss respondent decided that W.C. stood for
"Wayside Chapel." He wrote her that the W.C. was
situated nine miles from the house, in a grove of trees, and
was capable of holding more than 300 people — but was
open only Tuesdays, Thursdays and Sundays; during
tourist season, it was a good idea to go early and make a
day of it, especially on Sundays when there was an organ
accompaniment; the acoustics were wonderful: one could
hear the slightest sound.

The letter closed by saying that the writer wanted to
accommodate the lady in every possible way — and would
she like to reserve a seat up front or near the door?

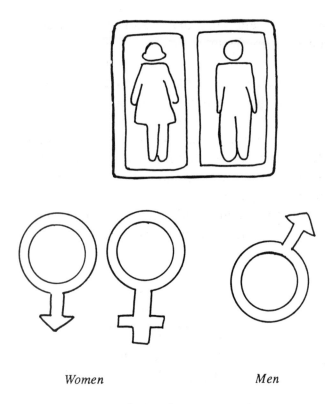

Women   *Men*

International signs for women and men

You should consult the language dictionary of the country you're visiting to learn the names for "toilet" and "men" and "women." Remember, *toilet* and *bathroom* are not the same. A bathroom is just that: a place to bathe.

Other than W.C., the toilet in Europe sometimes is called different things. The British refer to the toilet as the "loo." They will also sometimes say they want to "spend a penny;" this refers to a time when it cost a penny to use the toilet in England. That's not true, anymore.

In Ireland a friend didn't know the local words for men and women and relied on what he considered logic. To him, the sign MNA was close to identifying the facility he needed. He was surprised: in Gaelic the word MNA means

women, not men — and DIR means men. Need I explain
what happened to my friend?

In Hawaii, you'll also find signs that may puzzle you.
Wahine is women; Kane is men.

I found new signs on the toilet doors of my airplane from
London to San Francisco. For as long as I can remember
there was a slot on the toilet doors of planes, and when the
toilet was in use a sign in the slot read "occupied," and
when not occupied, the slot read "vacant." But on the
toilet doors of the plane the new signs were simply:

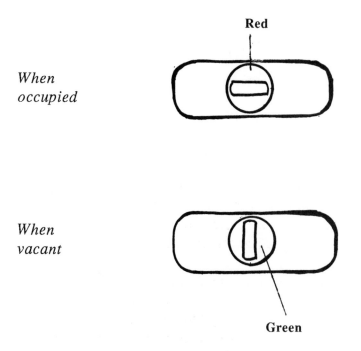

*When
occupied*

*When
vacant*

For hours, experienced travelers (including myself) tried
one by one to force open locked doors. By the end of the
eleven-hour journey, however, everyone seemed to have
figured out the meaning of these new red and green signs.

Toilet in Tanzania: Note signs for men and women

Lights and Mirrors

I have found that if there is a light in the toilet, the switch can be in unexpected places. Frequently it is *outside* the bathroom. There have been times when no amount of searching produced an obvious switch and the manager had to be called.

A traveling companion related a story about a toilet in a French restaurant. After he closed the door it became totally dark inside. He opened the door a crack to search for a light switch, but found none. Finally, he gave up and communicated the problem to the manager. To obtain light, he was told, close the door and turn the lock. Indeed, when the lock turned — the light came on!

Travelers should also be aware of problems with timer switches. In one small hotel on the Left Bank in Paris a couple ventured from their room the first night to search for the W.C. But the lights went out halfway down the hallway, and they retreated in darkness, fumbling for their room lock.

A second venture produced better results. One remained in the lighted room with the door open as the other scurried down the lighted hallway to the W.C. He arrived to flip the W.C. light just as the timed hall lights went out. For his return, there was light at the end of the tunnel: his partner was in their room with the doorway open.

In some parts of the world, travelers will find there is no electricity, or it is on for limited periods of time. In M'hamid, Morocco, a tiny village on the edge of the Sahara, our hotel had only four rooms, but there was a bathroom with running water. At 8 p.m., as I was scrubbing away the Sahara's sand in the shower, suddenly there were no lights: only total blackness. I knew the shower was only a few inches from the floor-level squat toilet, but I couldn't remember exactly where. I was reluctant to move lest I put my foot in something.

I was rescued when an alert porter heard my squeal of dismay and discreetly appeared at the door with a lighted candle. I later learned that the town's electricity came from a generator — which was turned off promptly at 8 p.m.

Because of problems abroad with toilet lights I strongly recommend that you take along a small flashlight, complete with extra supplies of fresh batteries.

In many toilets abroad an additional word of advice: mirrors are often nonexistent or very small and of poor quality. If appearance is important, you will find it wise to carry a small mirror of your own.

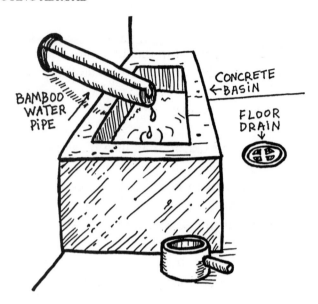

Asian bathroom: Use the dipper for bathing

Bathing Abroad

The subject of bathing is included in this book because many travelers think of the toilet and the bath as being in the same room — the bathroom.

Wrong. Bathing facilities in other countries vary and are frequently in separate places from the toilets. Taking a bath can be quite different abroad because many places do not have enough water for soaking baths, so travelers are limited to "bird" baths — quick washups from sinks — or taking simple showers. Hot water is scarce.

A simple bathing method, frequently referred to as an Indian bath (but in use in many countries), is one in which water is placed in a water-holding container, small as a plastic bucket, or big as a built-in concrete trough. These containers, however large, are not for submerging the body. You stand next to the container and pour water from it over your body with a dipper.

In the illustration on the previous page, water can be introduced into the basin by the management's pouring water into a pipe from the outside. Because there is no internal plumbing, much work is saved by not having to carry the water into the house.

The usual technique for taking a bath in these facilities is:

Step 1: Fill the dipper with water and wet your body.

Step 2: Put the dipper to one side and soap your body (Note: bring your own, for soap is often not supplied).

Step 3: Use the dipper to pour water over your body to rinse off the soap.

You may wonder where all this water will go. There will be a drain somewhere in the bathing room floor. Just pretend you are in a shower back home.

In the tropics bathing without hot water is refreshing, but when cold weather is encountered baths tend to be brief and will cover only the most essential areas. Be aware that asking for heated water may involve using precious and expensive wood, which you may be asked to pay for.

A simple bathing facility with running cold water

In cultures where bathing is done in a public place because of the lack of home facilities, washing up is accomplished while wearing clothing, such as a light sarong for women and shorts for men. Many travelers to these countries carry their own light cloth or sarong for bathing. It is not acceptable to bathe in the nude — or, for that matter, to stare at bathers.

You will find that many developing countries have some form of modern bathing facilities, as shown in the following illustrations. However, these bathrooms will differ from those most travelers are accustomed to at home.

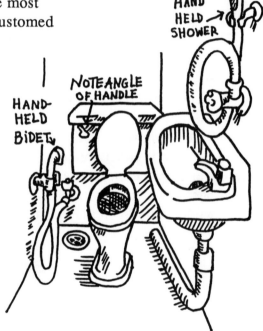

Compact modern bathroom abroad: Everything is at hand

The compact bathroom measures only three feet wide by five feet long. No toilet paper is provided, but the hand-held bidet is handily located beside the sit-type toilet; the movable hand-held shower attaches above the sink. Water from the shower and the sink splashes directly onto the floor; the drain is behind the toilet.

In the bathroom below, the sink drains by emptying water directly on the floor, which should slope to a corner drain.

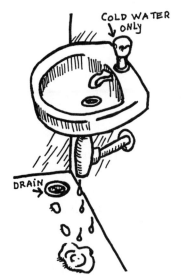

COLD WATER
↓ ONLY

DRAIN →

Look out below: Correct placement of your feet while using this sink can be important

If you are a traveler in a developing country, you would be wise to scrutinize the plumbing first — and then stand back from the sink with your feet spread wide apart to avoid getting soaked.

In some showers hot water is produced by an individual heater. You let water flow to the heating unit with the twist of a faucet handle. A simple on-off button turns the heater on; a temperature control knob rotates to give you a degree of warmth. Let it heat up. To use the shower, you remove the shower head from the holder and spray water on your body. It's a good idea to test the water temperature before you begin. If nothing happens, check elsewhere in the hotel room for a main power switch or circuit breaker for this unit.

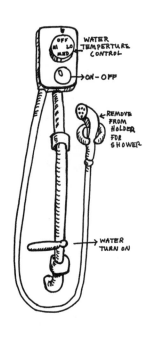

WATER TEMPERATURE CONTROL

→ ON - OFF

← REMOVE FROM HOLDER FOR SHOWER

→ WATER TURN ON

Individual heater warms water in this hand-held shower

You may have noticed there are no stoppers shown in the illustrations of sinks. This is because there usually are none! If you want a sink full of water, I suggest you carry a fit-all type stopper.

One of my favorite shower types abroad is one that often dominates the otherwise Western-style bathroom. The shower head is near the ceiling in the center of a small room and located between the toilet and sink.

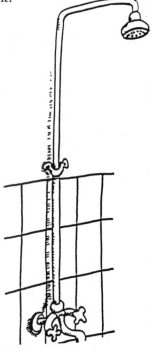

If you stand directly under it, the water will fall straight down on your head like a waterfall. Or you can stand next to the stream of shower water and manually splash it onto your body.

However, either approach results in wetting *everything* in the bathroom. Obviously all clothing, towels and personal effects will need to be left outside the door, and with foresight, within arm's reach.

Asian total immersion shower: With a few cautions, a favorite of the author

As usual, the water drain is somewhere in the corner of the room and, if you're lucky, the water will leave the floor fully within the next twelve hours.

Travelers may find unusual bathing arrangements aboard boats, such as this facility on a Brazilian vessel on the Amazon River. It's a combination toilet and shower in one very small room. Note the overhead shower nozzle.

To shower, one closes the toilet seat and turns on the shower water lever. This lets river water flow up the pipe to the shower head.

It's possible for hurried bathers to use the sit toilet and to shower at the same time. Care needs to be taken to correctly identify the toilet flusher and the shower water lever — or you might be in for a surprise.

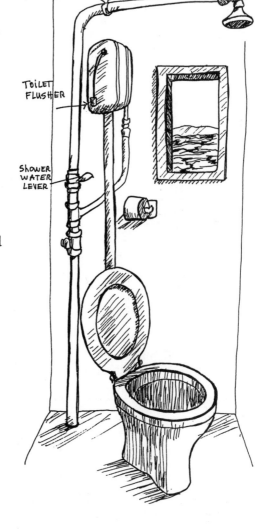

Take care with this boat's toilet and overhead shower combination, or you may get more than you counted on

Even in modern-appearing showers abroad, you frequently will find a bucket. This is a hint that the water pressure allows only a dribble of water and if you try to shower you will find it to be a frustrating affair. However, the water faucet below the shower may have good pressure and quickly fill the bucket — and you may find a bath from the bucket will be more to your liking.

Where's the toilet paper? In this five-star hotel in Salvador, Brazil, you have only to lift the lid of this cabinet — and voila!

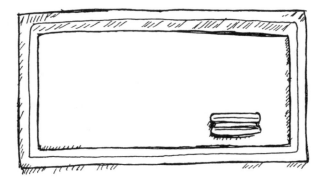

Hidden toilet paper holder

In the past, Turkey was famous for its public bathing facilities, but these are no longer what they once were because many homes now have their own private baths. The public baths are visited by those who have no facilities or who use them as a social meeting place. Men and women use the same facilities, but on different days.

Visiting a Turkish bath is still an interesting experience. You must first wash your body in a shower before actually entering the large hot pool-like bath. Your fellow bathers, at least in the women's bath, are usually friendly and your visit can be an occasion for a cultural exchange. For an additional fee an attendant will give you a massage.

Urinals

A urinal is an upright wall fixture used by men and seldom seen by women. It's mostly found in public men's toilets, but in some developing countries urinals can also be found in public unisex toilets.

Basically, urinals allow a standing male to urinate without removing his clothing. He need only unbutton or unzip his fly, pull out the private part needed for the job, and blaze away. The whole procedure is quite rapid and does away with the need for a stall toilet. Because of urinals, the lines at men's toilets can move briskly along, while women wait impatiently to use the more cumbersome stall toilets. The urinal also conserves resources since it only requires a small amount of water to flush.

Individual urinals in a row

Urinals come in various shapes and sizes. The most common is the individual urinal, mounted in a row along a wall, which a man can walk up to. It can be metal or molded plastic, but usually is ceramic. At the top is a hand flushing device or an automatic flusher.

In some cases, particularly abroad, the urinal can be an entire wall of the men's room, sheathed in galvanized metal, with a metal trough at the bottom sloping to a common drain. Some European urinals lack flushing water and are packed in ice in winter, which provides an interesting target for men doing their duty. These same men's rooms often have elderly female attendants, which do not make local males nervous.

Privacy is generally lacking, but no one seems to mind, provided a certain unwritten etiquette is followed. If the urinals are in use, the waiting males form a line along a wall well behind those who are busy. Approaching the urinal, a man unzips his fly only at the last minute. He then stares dutifully ahead while attending to his business, scrupulously avoiding staring at any other man's private parts or making eye contact. Conversation among strangers while urinating is considered rude and improper. And two gentlemen never use the same single urinal at once.

Toilet Tidbit

In Paris, if you should be lucky enough to locate the only public toilet in large department store, do not be surprised to find that women must pass through the men's section to reach their stalls. The sink and washing of hands area is shared. This arrangement is often found in restaurant restrooms — and doesn't seem to bother the French.

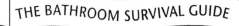

BRIEF HISTORY OF TOILETS

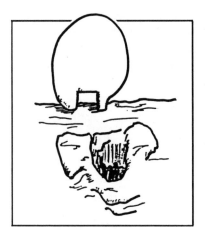

Toilet made of raw clay in Egyptian desert

**Tiptoe through the ages with us
to peek at mankind's
struggle to perfect the toilet**

The ancient Egyptians used sit toilets with a pot below to collect waste matter. Sand was probably used for cleaning, instead of water.

The Palace at Knossos in Crete (1400 BC) has a sit toilet and sewer system — in fact, a flushing toilet.

The Romans were masters of plumbing. They had public and private sit latrines that were flushed with water. The Romans were not concerned with privacy in these facilities.

I found a very good example of a Roman public toilet in some ruins in Tunisia, once a wealthy Roman outpost. Marble seats lined three sides of the building. Water ran in a trench under the seats. It is possible that the Romans used water for cleansing after using the toilet. Soap was unknown.

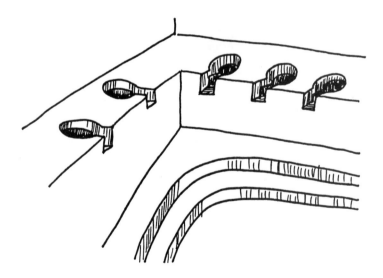

Remains of Roman toilet in Tunisia, complete with marble seats

After the Roman empire collapsed, there were no more baths or facilities for proper sewage disposal in Europe for a thousand years. In contrast, Constantinople continued to have a regular system of sanitation and, with an abundant water supply, their baths were famous.

Some interest in sanitation and personal bathing returned to Europe in the Middle Ages with the Crusaders, who had been in the Middle East.

In medieval times, privies called garderobes were often cantilevered from atop thick castle walls (some can be seen in old English castles). There were usually two or three seats in a bench, which opened to the moat (and the view) below. The effluence sometimes ran down the walls of the castle.

Castle garderobe:
Look out below

If no river or moat was available, there might be a pit or removable barrel under the toilet to collect the human waste. Public toilets were rare.

Even in London until the 1700s there was no running water in homes and no public fountains. Water was carried from wells or rivers. Chamber pots were common; night soil was collected for use by the farmers. Sometimes the night soil was simply thrown on the street to be picked up by farmers. In contrast, at this time, the royal court in India had a marble latrine that flushed with water.

In the past, privacy apparently was not desired. After social dinners, sometimes all the guests would retire to the latrine to continue the conviviality. Visits to the toilet were also a family affair. Pit toilets with holes enough for the entire family were common from the 1700s until fairly recent times. Apparently, the concept of privacy did not even begin until the 1800s.

The first modern flush water closet was designed in 1589 by Englishman John Harrington. However, it did not come into use until the late 1700s. A valve released the flow of water into the toilet. In the mid-1800s, another Englishman, Thomas Crapper, developed the flush toilet siphon system still in use in modern toilets. It is from this Englishman's name that the phrase came into being: "I'm going to visit the Crapper."

Only upper-class homes had water closets. Most everyone else used simple toilets such as the earth closet, which had a wooden seat with a bucket beneath. At the back was a hopper filled with dry dirt or ashes, which were dropped over the excrement. When the bucket was full, it was removed from the home to be emptied.

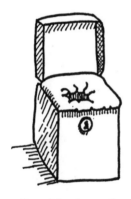

Furniture-holding earth closets were sometimes designed to hide the fact that inside was a toilet. At left is a royal bucket-type toilet, dating from the 1700s. Lift the lid, and there's the royal crapper.

Royal bucket toilet

Some furniture was also used to disguise other toilet items, such as this bidet (right), dating from the 1800s. It looked like an ordinary hassock, until the top was removed.

Bidet disguised as hassock

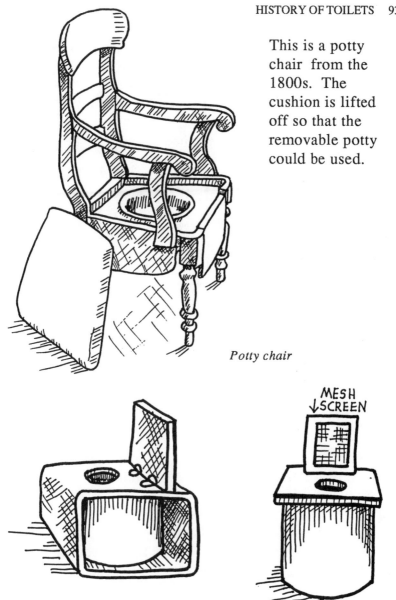

This is a potty chair from the 1800s. The cushion is lifted off so that the removable potty could be used.

Potty chair

Two types of can toilet, with lids

Wonder where the name *The Can* came from? These are examples of early can toilets (circa 1915) recommended by the U.S. Health Department. They could be built for $1. They also gave rise to the expression: Going to visit the can.

REMOVABLE
CAN

Turn of the century can-type outhouse

Heads up: Here's a design for an early 1900s outhouse with removable can for easy cleaning. This can-toilet was recommended by the U.S. Health Department as being more sanitary than the pit toilet. A requirement for a sanitary privy was a water-tight receptacle such as a pail, can, tub, barrel, tank or vault. Drying powders such as lime, dry earth and ashes were recommended for preventing disagreeable odors. A teacup of drying powder was to be sprinkled on each stool. Splashing in cans could be prevented by dropping a piece of thick paper or small pieces of wood on top of the cans' contents. Freezing and bursting of the cans had to be guarded against.

The pit privy, in common usage in the early years, was essentially a hole in the ground over which a privy house was built. When the pit was full, the house was moved to a new pit and the old pit was covered with soil. Soil pollution was a problem with this type of privy.

The lack of sewage systems was common into the 1940s in the rural areas of the United States Before 1920 few houses had bathrooms built in. Even in the 1950s, in some parts of this country, not everyone had baths.

In the early 1900s the development of the septic tank was considered an advancement for use in unsewered areas. Septic tanks are watertight storage tanks that hold household sewage while it decomposes by bacterial action. Septic tanks provide sewage treatment and a means for discharging the sewage with few health risks.

My eighty-five year old aunt described a trip in 1935 across the United States by car. She and her friends stayed nights in tourist cabins equipped with chamber pots. A young man would come each morning with a cart to collect the chamber pots.

A common facility at one time: A chamber pot under the bed

In England, at one time, outhouses were in wide use. *Netty* is the name euphemistically used for the outhouses that were common at the end of the garden in working-class English homes.

One variation is the wheelbarrow toilet that was used in a village near the sea. The toilet was located in the house, and a door opened from the outside of the house so that a wheel-barrow could be placed under the toilet. At the end of the week, the wheelbarrow was wheeled to the sea and cleaned. New sand was placed in the bottom and the wheelbarrow was returned to its spot under the toilet opening.

Old loos (toilets) have recently come into vogue again in Great Britain. To help their return, the English Heritage Organization arranges grants to repair outside toilets that are part of heritage houses, and England is full of these old houses!

Squat Toilets

No one knows when the squat toilet first appeared. Apparently it is an unsung accomplishment of mankind: I could find no published history of the squat toilet.

No doubt the squat toilet was in use from the beginning of civilization. The wealthy in societies probably had elegant versions of the squat toilet, much as Europeans did with their sit toilets.

Because of the squat toilet's simplicity of function, its basic design apparently has changed very little over the centuries.

MORE TOILET STORIES FROM ABROAD

Unique Chinese urinal
220 - 581 A.D.

**Further adventures
in the wide world
of toilets**

JAPAN

Japan is the home of the high-tech toilet. The simple toilets and bathing facilities of the Western World must be a real surprise to a Japanese traveler.

High-tech Japanese toilet

To use a Japanese toilet, you must master a panel with many buttons, all labeled in Japanese. When I visited Japanese homes, I inquired about their use and I was firmly instructed not to touch the controls on the panel. Apparently, it is common for foreigners to do the wrong thing with the buttons — sometimes with unusual results.

From what I could learn, using the panel takes skill. There is a button for cleaning a woman's frontal anatomy and another for a man's. Another button does the job for one's rear.

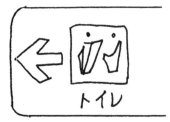

Japanese sign for a public toilet. The women's side is red and the men's in blue.

That's not all. There are buttons to control the water pressure and the temperature. Most homes and some public facilities have heated toilet seats, and, there is a button for that. (For more on the combination Japanese toilet and bidet, see page 60)

Toilet footwear also is specialized. Shoes are removed when you enter a Japanese home, and you are given a pair of slippers. But when you go into the toilet, which is a separate room from the bath, there will be a pair of slippers to be used only in the toilet.

Remove any slippers you have on and put on the toilet slippers. Do not leave the toilet with them on your feet — remember to leave them in the toilet.

Bathing involves more techniques to be strictly observed. There will be a shower and a very large tub filled with hot water in a room separate from the toilet. The tub usually has a cover to retain the heat. One must very carefully shower before entering the tub, which is not for bathing but soaking away stiff joints and the cares of the day.

Japanese toilet slippers
for use only in the toilet

The household follows an order in which each member of the family enters the tub, usually beginning with the man of the house and ending with the women. Guests are often given first choice.

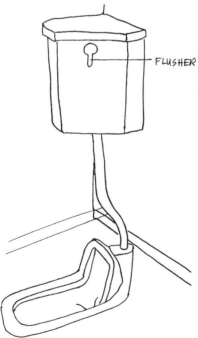

Toilet paper is usually provided in public facilities, but not always. Sometimes there is a machine at the entrance to the facility in which you can buy toilet paper. Have coins handy.

Paper towels for use after washing your hands are almost never provided. Most Japanese people prefer to carry a large handkerchief with them to use to dry their

A Japanese squat toilet
with a flusher

The Japanese bath is for soaking, not cleaning. It is unusually full of hot water with a cover to conserve heat.

hands and to also use as a napkin. This is why large pieces of beautiful handkerchief-like items are sold everywhere.

Of course, there are electric hot-air hand dryers available in some of the better places. When this convenience is around, it is usually in company with the latest in posh high-tech equipment.

PLACE yOUR HAND OVER The Sensor to FLush The ToiLeT

SeNSoR

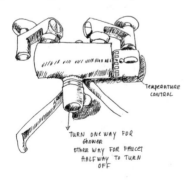

TeMPeRATURE CONTROL

TURN ONe WAY FOR
SHoweR
OTheR WAY FOR FAUCeT
HALF WAY To TURN
OFF

Shower faucet controls   *A Japanese high-tech flusher in a train. To use, place your hand over the sensor*

NORTH VIETNAM

North Vietnam is the land of truly creative toilets. No two seemed to be exactly alike and people simply did the logical thing in creating these toilets.

*Back of farm toilet
which houses urinal*

Although rapidly developing into a modern country, North Vietnam still is a land of contrasts. A traveler must be prepared for anything — from the comforts of modern toilet facilities in Hanoi to using the bushes in the country.

Outside of Hanoi, restaurants tend to be small, family businesses, usually located in a front room of their living quarters. The toilet will be the family's toilet and you sometimes will find creative toilet facilities, usually not of the flush kind.

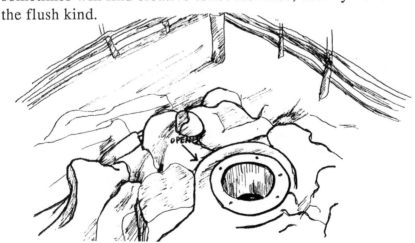

*A North Vietnamese farm toilet utilizing a large metal pipe is
conveniently located on rocks.*

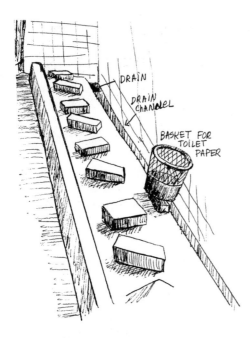

Sometimes, looking for a toilet is an adventure. In one case, we stopped at a small village for supper after heavy rains turned the countryside into mud --- gooey stuff several inches thick.

In this modern Vietnamese public toilet (women's side), urinals consist of strategically placed stones upon which women squat. A drain channel near the wall carries away fluids; a basket is propped up over a stone to received used toilet paper.

The toilet was outside and located at the top of a steep slope of goo. After a laborious climb in the dark, we found the toilet, complete with the usual straw screen --- with several boards with a strategic gap between them placed over a small ditch. Mud covered all, and soon, traveler's bottoms as well.

A less modern public toilet has a simple trench, with drain near the wall, over which participants squat. On right is a vat of water for cleansing.

Toilet signs of the times: In Vietnam, toilet signs for men say nam and women nu, and the WC is either WC or ve sinh.

Vietnamese farmers carrying night soil to use in the fields. The man has a straw hat and straw buckets.

North Vietnamese like to separate toilet functions. While visiting a lovely old farmhouse I checked out their toilet facilities. Near the house was a two-sided straw screen shielding the urinal. Two large rocks had been positioned for the feet.

Much further up a steep slope was a three-sided straw structure with a roof. The natural position of the rocks had been utilized for the placement of the feet. Of course this was a squat toilet. The rocks also created a trench and a large metal pipe had been positioned over the trench to create a toilet bowl for bowel movements. The debris was later scraped up and utilized as fertilizer. I noted the cabbages in the fields were exceptionally large.

This is a urinal and bathhouse for a farmer.

Here's an innovative toilet for a restaurant — a single wooden log, with an appropriate hole, cantilevered with bamboo poles over a handy river. Rags and plastic screen provide some privacy.

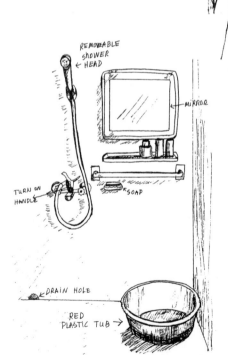

In a North Vietnamese hotel, the shower stall consists of a large plastic tub in the bathroom next to the toilet. Frequently bright red in color, the tub is about two feet in diameter. For the Vietnamese who are accustomed to bathing from a bucket, this is a very generous bathing facility.

Typical modern Vietnamese shower has shower head on a hose and a small plastic tub. There's a drain hole in the wall.

You can simply fill the tub and stand it in to bathe. Or you can use the portable shower head and spray yourself. The water can be used to flush the toilet. The choices are yours to make.

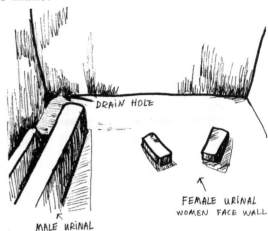

In the Vietnamese unisex toilet, there is a squat facility in a stall, with or without a door. The bricks form the female urinal, with the women facing the wall. On the left is the male urinal, which drains to a hole in the wall.

Toilet fact: Don't be surprised to find used toothbrushes and combs in bathrooms. These are left by polite Vietnamese travelers for use by the next visitors.

CRETE

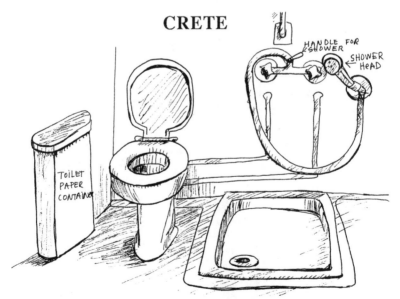

Typical bathroom arrangement in a hotel in Crete. You stand in the large pan and position the shower head as needed. Beside the toilet is a large can. This is for your used toilet paper.

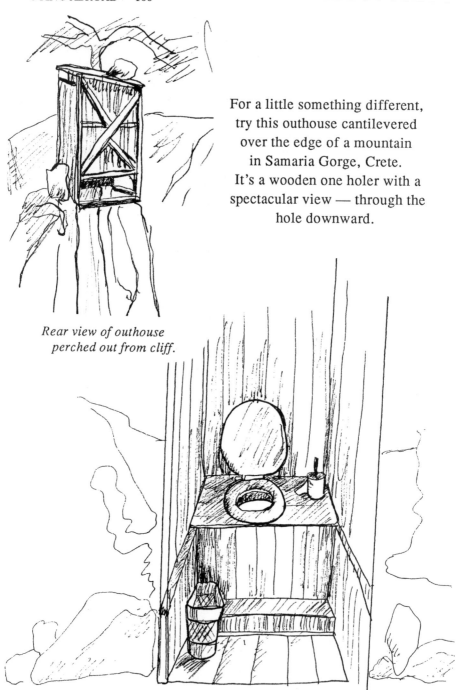

For a little something different,
try this outhouse cantilevered
over the edge of a mountain
in Samaria Gorge, Crete.
It's a wooden one holer with a
spectacular view — through the
hole downward.

*Rear view of outhouse
perched out from cliff.*

*Interior view. Peek through the hole for a special view
(and hope that when you use it no one below is looking up).*

Here's an innovative toilet found on the trail in Samaria Gorge, Crete. It's a squat toilet (the feet go in the ridged area) and the tall device with a large can at the top is the water flusher.

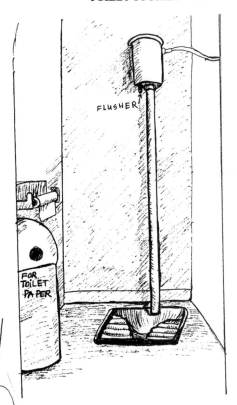

FLUSHER

FOR TOILET PAPER

In a stone hut on a trail in Imbros Gorge, Crete, the facility is a squat toilet. The bucket of water on the right is for flushing t he toilet; the can on the left is for collecting used toilet paper. Do not throw toilet paper down the toilet.

WATER TANK

FOR FLUSHING TOILET

FOR TOILET PAPER

YEMEN

Toilets in Yemen can be different from any you have ever seen. However, in this desert country where water is scarce, the Yemen toilets are practical.

Though the houses have lavoratories on all floors, the soil pipes are joined in a vertical shaft leading down to a masonry pit under the house. There is a door to remove the debris for use as fertilizer.

Liquids pass through another vertical channel outside the walls. These concrete channels usually are situated on the north side of the house.

Beside the toilet, a bathroom contains a place for bathing and another for general ablation. Water is carried into the house in large jars that are placed in the bathroom. The bathroom walls are made of hard gypsum so they easily can be cleaned.

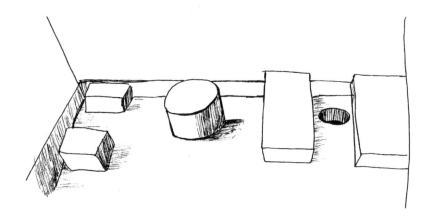

A starkly functional Yemen bath and toilet. The hole on the right marks the squat toilet. The blocks on the left are for standing upon while bathing.

A view of the Chinese community farm toilet. The working end is the shallow toilet trench (right) which one straddles. On the left is an open four-foot deep pit, into which the trench drains.

CHINA

China has a variety of toilets (also see p. 30), including a number of public toilets with a trench over which the participants straddle and squat. Privacy is non-existent.

On my last trip to China, I visited a country village where I was introduced to their new public toilet. They were very proud. The community toilet is a concrete building complete with walls and a roof. One squats over a shallow toilet trench, which runs at right angles to a four-foot deep pit. Debris drains from the sloped trench directly into the toilet pit.

The unisex facility has no privacy at all. One would not want to fall into the toilet pit. Luckily, I was there on a cool day, but on a hot day, the smell must be overwhelming.

Layout of the farm toilet. One squats over the trench.

A variation on the Chinese trench toilet. It consists of a hole with small partitions on either side, for a little privacy from your neighbors (but none in front or back).

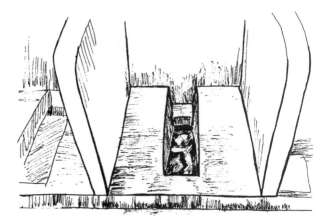

A friend recently told me about her trip to China and her first experience with the Chinese trench toilet. When she was first introduced to the facility, she thought it was, er, so public, that she was reluctant to use it.But her need was pressing, and as she arranged herself and straddled the trench, she found that local women had gathered in a crowd to watch her. This she found distressing, but even

Sign for Chinese toilet

worse, when she stood up after she had finished, the crowd of women seemed pleased ---- and applauded

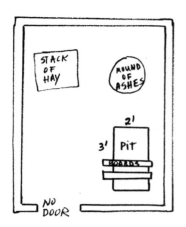

Layout of recycling farm toilet for private use. Boards cover a pit, over which the participant squats. After use, debris in pit is covered with ashes and hay. When the pit is full, debris is removed to be used in the fields as fertilizer.

ICELAND

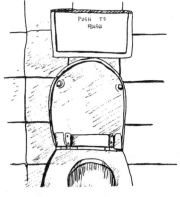

If you are looking for a toilet, the word is *snyrting*, and for men, look for *kalar*, and women, *konur*. The signs indicating toilets are fairly common, but you will not see the word, toilet. Many toilets have an Icelandic water saver flusher and

A lot or a litle?

give you a choice of flushes. Light flush is on the right; a hearty, full flush is on the left.

Use your head. The unit above the toilet is the flusher.

Here's a handy toilet located off the back stairs of an Icelandic bus. Open the door, and step inside: there's a compact but usable facility.

INDIA

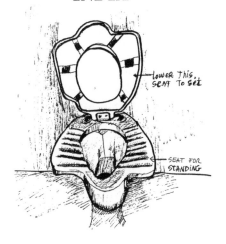

You can either sit or stand on this toilet in India. To use the facility as a squat toilet, raise the seat and place your feet upon the porcelain. Squat. To use as a Western-style toilet, lower the seat, lower yourself and sit.

AUSTRALIA

In Australia, if you are looking for the toilet facilities, ask for the "dunnies." The designation simply can read "male" or "female," but also "blokes" for men and "sheilas" for women.

Little or big flush?

Unless you are far in the bush, where there are only bushes for toilets, Australian facilities are usually quite ordinary Western flush toilets. The only difference I found were the conservation of water flush mechanisms. These are usually on top of the tank and have two buttons. Press the half circle for a partial flush and the full circle for a full flush.

TOILET TIDBITS

A friend reported his wife's reaction to her first squat toilet encounter in a campground in France. Breathless, she rushed from the women's restroom. "They've taken out the equipment," she said, incredulously.

Something you always wanted to know: In the earth's northern hemisphere, the water in a toilet bowl moves clockwise. In the southern hemisphere, the water circulates counter clockwise.

In the beautiful countryside of Romania, the toilets are largely outhouses. Old newspapers are cut into squares and used as toilet paper. It also gives one some reading matter.

In the International Airport in Amsterdam, the urinals are painted with very realistic flies. Perhaps to help with the aim?

THOUGHTS
AT THE END

**A few parting words about
staying well while abroad —
and keeping that
essential attitude**

Tips on staying well

In many countries, you must be especially careful about the food you eat — or else you may spend more time than you had planned in the local facility.

I am not a health authority, but I have avoided diarrhea and other intestinal distress by taking a few simple health precautions. I also get a gamma globulin (Hepatitis) shot before traveling. there is now a vaccination for Hepatitis A that is good for ten years.

I generally consider it unsafe to eat anything that has been washed in the local water, such as salads and unpeeled fruit. A good idea is to confine your eating to piping hot food, fresh from the stove.

In some developing countries dishwashing facilities usually lack hot enough water to sanitize the plates, glasses and utensils; even the source of the water may be questionable. Don't drink tap water and do not brush your teeth in it. Ice made of local water may also be contaminated. Use bottled water, which is widely available. If its cost bothers you, remember that it is cheaper than becoming ill. You must consider adding the cost of bottled water to your necessary travel expenses.

Before you buy, check the water bottle to be certain it has a good seal. A bottle that leaks is unsuitable, as is one that is partially full. A loose cap can mean trouble — that it has been refilled, and perhaps not with pure water.

Clean your hands well before eating or putting your hands near your mouth. Memorize and follow the precautions on pages 8 and 9 of this book.

Before going abroad, visit your physician to stock up on necessary medications, take recommended injections, and learn about precautions you must take.

For more information, check The Centers for Disease Control and Prevention (CDC) web site at:

http://www. cdc.gov/travel/

This informative site provide health information on specific destinations and what you need to know before you go. Included is information on outbreaks of concern to international travelers, tips on traveling with children, how to avoid illness from food or water as well as vaccination recommendations.

The CDC also maintains a Traveler's Health Hotline with recorded messages on current health risks, suggested immunizations and food/water precautions.

The toll-free telephone number is *877-FYI-TRIP.*

The toll-free fax number for requesting information is *888-232-3299.* The fax information is also available on the CDC web site.

The Importance of Attitude

I think that one's attitude toward travel is very important. Travel to many countries, particularly developing ones, will expose you to life styles different than your own. This is what is interesting about such travel. It challenges your senses with new and different experiences; you will learn new and interesting ways to see the world.

But you must be prepared to adjust. Obviously, you will face unusual situations; things can and will go wrong.

Remember travel is fun (and you spent a lot of money to do this). Keep uppermost in mind that you are a guest in someone else's country.

Later on, when you exchange stories with fellow travelers, you will find that the stories retold with relish are those in which you faced hardships or difficulties. The easy, carefree travels are the ones that are first to be forgotten. You may also be surprised to discover that "adventure" travel can become addictive.

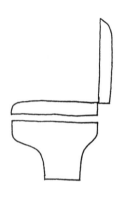

Japanese sign for
Western-type toilet

At a recent party a friend demonstrated the kind of attitude I think is needed for travel. She remarked that she found the toilets more interesting than the beds. Beds, she claimed, are more or less the same everywhere — but toilets are often a real surprise.

In conclusion, I hope that your travels will be easier with the information and attitudes given to you in this book.

Having a good time while traveling is often not so much an absence of problems as the ability to deal with them. Remember that few things in life can make you feel badly unless you let them.

One is not born a traveler; one learns how to become one. Lead with a good attitude and the rest will follow.

Good luck and happy traveling wherever you, er, go.

ACKNOWLEDGMENTS

TO Ken Hughes, who gave me courage to attempt the deed
and shared his expertise and time so generously.

TO George Narita, who said I should DO IT.

TO Connie Diernisse, who provided time, hard work, and stories.

TO Claudia Davison, who provided excellent ideas and encouragement.

TO Ronald and Valerie Montes, who gave endless help,
information and support.

TO Sam Moorman, for saving my efforts.

TO Joe Walton, who provided hard work.

TO Nichole Sparks, who provided nimble fingers
and computer expertise.

And to all my friends, with whom I have shared travels
and who have shared their stories with me:

Thelma Rubin
Iona Ali
Naomi Baird
Shirley Dietderich
Karen Johnson
Bert Verrips
Benny Alba
and Alberta Jackson Epsie

BIBLIOGRAPHY

Horan, Julie L. *The Porcelain God: A Social History of the Toilet.* Secaucus, N.J.: Birch Lane Press, 1996.

Howarth, Jane W. *Healthy Travel: Bugs, Bites & Bowels.* Old Saybrook, CT: Globe Pequot Press. 1995.

Kira, Alexander. *The Bathroom.* New York: Viking Press, 1976.

Murphy, Joseph E. *South to the Pole by Ski.* St. Paul, MN: Marlor Press, 1990.

Zakowich, Paul. *Culture Shock. A Traveller's Medical Guide.* Portland, OR: Graphic Arts Center Publishing, 1995.

INDEX

"An open mind for the mysteries of the world's toilets is always helpful — and if you can't figure it out, you can always ask, you know." — Eva Newman

Self-portrait of Eva in her favorite fold-up travel hat

Author Eva Newman is a former social worker who lives in Oakland, California. An artist as well as a writer, she enjoys traveling to out-of-the-way places of the world and these days pretty much takes any toilet she finds in stride.